Biology for the Grammar Stage

Teacher Guide

Biology for the Grammar Stage Teacher Guide

Updated Edition, 2nd Printing

Email: support@elementalscience.com

ISBN # 978-1-935614-30-2

Printed in the USA for worldwide distribution
Pictures by Paige Hudson and Erin Simons (One Line Design)

For more copies write to:
Elemental Science
PO Box 79
Niceville, FL 32588
support@elementalscience.com

Copyright Policy

Biology for the Grammar Stage Teacher Guide Table of Contents

Biology for the Grammar Stage
Introduction to the Updated Edition

Since writing the first edition of *Biology for the Grammar Stage,* I have co-authored *Success in Science: A Manual for Excellence in Science Education* with Bradley Hudson. The purpose of this updated edition was to re-align this program with our research. It now reflects the components of the Classic Method of elementary science instruction suggested in the book. This method is loosely based on the ideas for classical science education that are laid out in *The Well-trained Mind: A Guide to Classical Education at Home* by Jessie Wise and Susan Wise Bauer.

In *Success in Science,* we compare the elementary student to an empty bucket that is waiting to be filled with meaningful information. My goal in writing this curriculum was to provide you with tools to give your elementary student exposure to the topics of animals, the human body and plants, thus building a knowledge base for future studies. For this reason, I have included weekly scientific demonstrations, reading suggestions, notebooking assignments, and additional activities.

This program is designed to be used during the elementary years, specifically 1st through 4th grade. It includes a buffet of options that can be completed in either two days or five days each. Alternatively, if you desire, you could set aside an hour a week to be your science day in which you do all the readings, narrations, and activities planned for the week. Please feel free to act as the student's scribe as you complete the narration pages and lab reports.

Student Workbook (SW)

This teacher's guide is designed to work in conjunction with the *Biology for the Grammar Stage Student Workbook.* This workbook is sold separately, but it is critical to the success of this program. It contains all the pages you will need to complete the narrations, lab reports, and multi-week projects. The student workbook gives the students the ability to create a lasting memory of their first journey through biology.

Scientific Demonstrations

The scientific demonstrations scheduled in the guide generally use easy to find materials and tie into what is being studied. Each one has a corresponding lab report in the student workbook. At this age, you will be the driving force behind these demonstrations, meaning that you will be the one in control and the student will be watching and participating when necessary. These demonstrations are designed to give them a beginners' look at the scientific method and how scientific tests work. It is not necessary to ask them to predict the outcome of the demonstration as they have no knowledge base to determine what the answer should be. However, if the students enjoy predicting or they are able to tell you what will happen, please feel free to let them do so.

Each lab report includes four sections:

1. The "Our Tools" section is for the materials that were used during the demonstration.

2. The "Our Method" section is for a brief description of what was done during the scientific demonstration. This should be in the students words.
3. The "Our Outcome" section is for what the students observed during the demonstration.
4. The "Our Insight" section is for what the students learned from the scientific demonstration.

Any time you see a box for a picture on the lab report you can have the students draw what happened or you can take a picture of the demonstration and glue it in the box. For younger students, I recommend that you do most (if not all) the writing for them on the lab reports.

Science-oriented Books

The science-oriented books section includes reading assignments from encyclopedias, discussion questions, and additional books for every lesson. Each of the reading assignments should be read with the students or, if they are capable, have them read the assignments on their own. After the reading assignment is completed, discuss the topic with the students using the provided discussion questions. These questions are meant to help them begin to gather their thoughts in preparation for giving a narration.

In this edition of *Biology for the Grammar Stage,* I have also included a list of additional books for you to choose from each week. These are meant to be checked out from the library, and are not necessary to the success of this program. It is there in case you decide that you would like to dig a little deeper into the topics. I have done my best to choose in-print, widely available books, but since every library is different, the books listed may not be available in your area. If that is the case, simply look up the topic in your local card catalog.

Notebooking

For the notebooking component, you will ask the students to narrate what they have learned from the science-oriented books. They should add their narration to their student workbook. For younger students I recommend that you have them dictate what they have learned to you and then you write this into their student workbook. You can also have the students copy their narration into the workbook. You only need to expect one to two sentences from a first or second grade student.

Next, have the students color the provided picture on the narration page. All the pages and pictures you need are included in the student workbook. I suggest that you read over these pages monthly so that the students get a review of what they have been learning. I have also included optional lapbook assignments in the case that your students prefer to use lapbooks over notebooking.

Finally, go over the vocabulary with the students and enter it into their glossary at the rear of the student workbook. You can write this for them, have them copy the definition, or dictate the definition to the students. If you choose to have the students look up the definitions, I have included a glossary of the terms in this program in the Appendix on pp. 202-204.

Multi-week Projects and Activities

This guide includes ideas for multi-week projects and additional activities that coordinate with each lesson. The pages and pictures needed for the multi-week projects are included in the student workbook, while the directions for creating them are found in this guide. The additional activities include crafts and other activities that can enhance the students' learning time. There are no sheets to record these additional activities in the student workbook. However, I have included a project record sheet template on pg. 206 of the Appendix of this guide.

Memorization

The elementary student is very capable of receiving and memorizing information. With this in mind, I recommend that you capitalize on this fact by having your students memorize the included vocabulary and basic facts related to biology. A list of simple poems that you can use to help them memorize the characteristics of animals, plants, and the body systems is included on the unit overview sheet of each unit. Remember that these poems are included as a resource for you to augment students' learning experience and they are not required to use this program successfully.

Possible Schedules

I have written this updated edition to contain a buffet of activities that you can choose from when guiding the students through their first look at biolgy. This gives you, the teacher, complete freedom in what you would like to utilize to present and explore the concepts each week. However, I have also included two potential schedules for you to give an idea of how you could schedule each week. You can choose to use these as your guide or create your own. I have included two schedule templates on pp. 207-208 of the Appendix of this guide for you to use.

Quizzes

We have also created a set of weekly quizzes to use with this program, which can be found at the back of the student workbook. Although these quizzes are not essential, they are helpful in assessing how much the students are retaining. You can also use the quizzes as a review of what the students have studied by giving the quiz orally or by having the students fill each quiz out with the assistance of their workbooks. The correct answers for the quizzes are included at the end of each week in this guide.

Coordinating Products

The following products by Elemental Science coordinate with this program. These two eBooks are available separately through our website.

- ***Biology for the Grammar Stage Lapbooking Templates*** — We have created templates for four lapbooks to coordinate with *Biology for the Grammar Stage*. You can use these lapbooks as a means of review or in place of the student workbook. The directions for using these templates are found in this guide under the notebooking section.

- *Biology for the Grammar Stage Coloring Pages* — We have also created a set of coloring pages to use with this program. Although they are not essential, they are helpful for adding in younger students or for reinforcing key concepts for artistic students.

Helpful Articles

Our goal as a company is to provide you with the information you need to be successful in your quest to educate your student in the sciences at home. This is the main reason we share tips and tools for homeschool science education at our blogs. As you prepare to guide your students through this program, you may find the following articles helpful:

- ***Classical Science Curriculum for the Grammar Stage Student*** — This article explains the goals of grammar stage science and demonstrates how the classical educator can utilize the tools they have at their disposal to reach these goals.
  - http://elementalblogging.com/classical-science-curriculum-grammar/
- ***Scientific Demonstrations vs. Experiments*** — This article shares about these two types of scientific tests and points out how to employ scientific demonstrations or experiments in your homeschool.
  - http://elementalscience.com/blogs/news/89905795-scientific-demonstrations-or-experiments
- ***The Basics of Notebooking*** — This article clarifies what notebooking is and describes how this method can be a beneficial addition to your homeschool.
  - http://elementalblogging.com/the-basics-of-notebooking/

Additional Resources

The following page contains quick links to the activities suggested in this guide along with several helpful downloads:

- https://elementalscience.com/blogs/resources/bgs

Final Thoughts

As the author and publisher of this curriculum I encourage you to contact me with any questions or problems that you might have concerning *Biology for the Grammar Stage* at support@elementalscience.com. I will be more than happy to answer them as soon as I am able. You may also get additional help at our yahoo group (http://groups.yahoo.com/group/elemental_science/). I hope that you will enjoy *Biology for the Grammar Stage*!

Required Book List

The following books are scheduled for use in this guide. You will need to purchase them or find a suitable substitute to complete this program.

Encyclopedias

Animals Unit (Choose **one** age-appropriate option.)

- *Kingfisher First Encyclopedia of Animals (best for K through 2nd grade)* **OR**
- *DK Encyclopedia of Animals (best for 2nd through 4th grade)*

Human Body Unit (Choose **one** age-appropriate option.)

- *DK First Human Body Encyclopedia (best for 1st through 3rd grade)* **OR**
- *Kingfisher Science Encyclopedia (best for 4th through 6th grade)*

Plants Unit (Choose **one** age-appropriate option.)

- *Basher Science: Biology - Life as we know it! (best for 1st through 4th grade)* **OR**
- *Usborne Science Encyclopedia (best for 3rd through 5th grade)*

Scientific Demonstration Books

You will need both of these books to complete the scientific demonstrations in this program.

- *Janice VanCleave's Biology for Every Kid* **AND**
- *Janice VanCleave's Science Around the World*

Additional Books Listed by Week

The books listed below are completely optional! They are not required to complete this program. Instead, this list is merely a suggestion of the additional books that are available to enhance your studies. This list is by no means exhaustive.

Animals Unit

Animals Week 1

- *A Desert Habitat (Introducing Habitats)* by Kelley Macaulay and Bobbie Kalman
- *About Habitats: Deserts* by Cathryn P. Sill
- *Life in the Desert (Pebble Plus: Habitats Around the World)* by Alison Auch
- *A Grassland Habitat (Introducing Habitats)* by Kelley Macaulay and Bobbie Kalman
- *Grasslands (About Habitats)* by Cathryn P. Sill
- *A Savanna Habitat (Introducing Habitats)* by Bobbie Kalman
- *A Rainforest Habitat (Introducing Habitats)* by Molly Aloian

Animals Week 2

- *A Forest Habitat (Introducing Habitats)* by Bobbie Kalman
- *Northern Refuge: A Story of a Canadian Boreal Forest* by Audrey Fraggalosch
- *The Arctic Habitat (Introducing Habitats)* by Molly Aloian and Bobbie Kalman

- *Arctic Tundra (Habitats)* by Michael H. Forman
- *Arctic Tundra* by Donald M. Silver

Animals Week 3

- *What is a Mammal? (Science of Living Things)* by Kalman
- *Face to Face with Lions (Face to Face with Animals)* by Beverly Joubert
- *Tawny Scrawny Lion (Little Golden Book)* by Golden Books and Gustaf Tenggren
- *The Cheetah: Fast as Lightning (Animal Close-Ups)* by Christine Denis-Huot and Michel Denis-Huot
- *Cheetah (Welcome Books: Animals of the World)* by Edana Eckart
- *Cheetah Cubs: Station Stop 2 (All Aboard Science Reader)* by Ginjer L. Clarke and Lucia Washburn
- *Elephants: A Book for Children* by Steve Bloom
- *Face to Face With Elephants (Face to Face with Animals)* by Beverly Joubert

Animals Week 4

- *Zebras (Wild Ones)* by Jill Anderson
- *How the Zebra Got Its Stripes (Little Golden Book)* by Justine Fontes
- *Hippos (Naturebooks: Safari Animals)* by Jenny Markert
- *The Hiccupotamus* by Aaron Zenz
- *Fox* by Kate Banks
- *Foxes (Animal Predators)* by Sandra Markle

Animals Week 5

- *Giraffes* by Jill Anderson
- *Baby Giraffes (It's Fun to Learn about Baby Animals)* by Bobbie Kalman
- *Chee-Lin: A Giraffe's Journey* by James Rumford
- *Camels (Nature Watch (Lerner))* by Cherie Winner
- *I Wonder Why Camels Have Humps: And Other Questions About Animals* by Anita Ganeri
- *Deer (Animals That Live in the Forest)* by JoAnn Early Macken
- *Deer (Blastoff! Readers: Backyard Wildlife)* by Derek Zobel

Animals Week 6

- *Pi-Shu the Little Panda* by John Butler
- *Endangered Pandas (Earth's Endangered Animals)* by John Crossingham
- *Tracks of a Panda* by Nick Dowson
- *Face to Face with Polar Bears (Face to Face with Animals)* by Norbert Rosing and Elizabeth Carney
- *Polar Bears* by Mark Newman
- *Where Do Polar Bears Live? (Let's-Read-and-Find... Science 2)* by Sarah L. Thomson
- *The Chimpanzee Family Book (Animal Family Series)* by Jane Goodall
- *Endangered Chimpanzees (Earth's Endangered Animals)* by Bobbie Kalman

Animals Week 7

- *Kangaroo (Life Cycle of A...)* by Angela Royston

- *Kangaroo Island: A Story of an Australian Mallee Forest - a Wild Habitats Book* by Deirdre Langeland
- *Koala (Life Cycle of A...)* by Bobbie Kalman
- *A Koala Is Not a Bear! (Crabapples)* by Hannelore Sotzek
- *Beaver (Life Cycle of A...)* by Bobbie Kalman
- *Beavers* by Helen H. Moore
- *The Adventures of Buddy the Beaver: Buddy Explores the Pond* by Carson Clark and Jim Clark

Animals Week 8

- *Armadillos (Animals Underground)* by Emily Sebastian
- *Amazing Armadillos (Step into Reading)* by Jennifer Guess McKerley
- *Skunks (Animal Prey)* by Sandra Markle
- *Skunk's Spring Surprise* by Leslea Newman
- *Skunks (Blastoff! Readers: Backyard Wildlife)* by Emily K. Green
- *Rabbits (Blastoff! Readers: Backyard Wildlife)* by Derek Zobel
- *Rabbits and Raindrops* by Jim Arnosky
- *The Little Rabbit* by Judy Dunn
- *The Tale of Peter Rabbit* by Beatrix Potter

Animals Week 9

- *Little Walrus Warning (Smithsonian Oceanic Collection)* by Carol Young
- *Walruses (Blastoff! Readers: Oceans Alive)* by Colleen A. Sexton
- *Face to Face with Whales (Face to Face with Animals)* by Flip Nicklin
- *Amazing Whales! (I Can Read Book 2)* by Sarah L. Thomson
- *Is a Blue Whale the Biggest Thing There Is? (Robert E. Wells Science)* by Robert E. Wells
- *Face to Face with Dolphins (Face to Face with Animals)* by Flip Nicklin
- *Dolphin Talk: Whistles, Clicks, and Clapping Jaws (Let's-Read-and-Find...)* by Wendy Pfeffer
- *Eye Wonder: Whales and Dolphins* by Caroline Bingham

Animals Week 10

- *Goats (Animals That Live on the Farm)* by JoAnn Early Macken
- *Life on a Goat Farm (Life on a Farm)* by Judy Wolfman
- *Little Apple Goat* by Caroline Church
- *Cows and Their Calves (Pebble Plus: Animal Offspring)* by Margaret Hall
- *Raising Cows on the Koebels' Farm (Our Neighborhood)* by Alice K. Flanagan
- *Milk: From Cow to Carton (Let's-Read-and-Find... Book)* by Aliki
- *Pigs (Animals That Live on the Farm)* by JoAnn Early Macken
- *Life on a Pig Farm (Life on a Farm)* by Judy Wolfman
- *The Three Little Pigs*

Animals Week 11

- *Eagles (Animal Predators)* by Sandra Markle

- *Bald Eagles (Nature Watch (Lerner))* by Charlotte Wilcox
- *Challenger: America's Favorite Eagle* by Margot Theis Raven
- *The Barn Owl (Animal Lives)* by Bert Kitchen
- *White Owl, Barn Owl* by Michael Foreman and Nicola Davies
- *There's an Owl in the Shower* by Jean Craighead George
- *Parrots and Other Birds (Animal Survivors)* by Mary Schulte
- *Parrots (The World's Smartest Animals)* by Ruth Owen
- *Kakapo Rescue: Saving the World's Strangest Parrot (Scientists in the Field Series)* by Sy Montgomery

Animals Week 12

- *Face to Face with Penguins (Face to Face with Animals)* by Yva Momatiuk
- *Emperor Penguin (Life Cycle of A...)* by Bobbie Kalman
- *National Geographic Readers: Penguins!* by Anne Schreiber
- *From Egg to Chicken (How Living Things Grow)* by Anita Ganeri
- *Chickens Aren't the Only Ones (World of Nature Series)* by Ruth Heller
- *Chickens (Animals That Live on the Farm)* by JoAnn Early Macken
- *Ducks and Their Ducklings (Pebble Plus: Animal Offspring)* by Margaret Hall
- *Duck (Life Cycles)* by Louise Spilsbury

Animals Week 13

- *Swans (Early Bird Nature)* by Lynn M. Stone
- *Six Swans* by Brothers Grimm
- *The Ugly Duckling* by Hans Christian Anderson
- *Swallows In The Birdhouse* by Stephen R. Swinburne
- *The Journey of a Swallow (Lifecycles)* by Carolyn Scrace
- *Swallow (Animal Neighbors)* by Stephen Savage
- *Hummingbirds (Welcome to the World Series)* by Diane Swanson
- *The Bee Hummingbird (Animals of Americas)* by Emma Romeu
- *Hummingbirds: Facts and Folklore from the Americas* by Jeanette Larson

Animals Week 14

- *Flamingos (Safari Animals)* by Maddie Gibbs
- *A Flamingo Chick Grows Up (Baby Animals (Learner Classroom))* by Joan Hewett
- *The Life Cycle of a Flamingo (Things With Wings)* by JoAnn Early Macken
- *The Peacock's Pride* by Melissa Kajpust
- *Peacocks, Penguins, and Other Birds (Animal Kingdom Classification series)* by Steve Parker
- *How the Peacock Got Its Feathers: Based on a Mayan Tale (Latin American Tales and Myths)* by Sandy Sepehri
- *Ostriches (Safari Animals)* by Maddie Gibbs
- *Ostriches (Animals That Live in the Grasslands)* by Therese Harasymiw
- *Can You Tell an Ostrich from an Emu? (Lightning Bolt Books: Animal Look-Alikes)* by

Buffy Silverman

Animals Week 15

- *Chameleons (Animals of the Rainforest)* by Erika Deiters and Jim Deiters
- *Chameleons and Other Animals with Amazing Skin (Scholastic News Nonfiction Readers)* by Susan LaBella
- *The Mixed-up Chameleon* by Eric Carle
- *101 Facts About Iguanas* by Sarah Williams
- *Iguanas (The World of Reptiles)* by Sophie Lockwood
- *I Wanna Iguana* by Karen Kaufman Orloff
- *What's Inside a Rattlesnake's Rattle? (Kids' Questions)* by Heather Montgomery
- *Rattlesnakes (Animal Predators)* by Sandra Markle
- *Baby Rattlesnake* by Lynn Moroney

Animals Week 16

- *Who Lives in an Alligator Hole? (Let's-Read-and-Find... Science 2)* by Anne Rockwell
- *What's the Difference Between an Alligator and a Crocodile? (What's the Difference? (Capstone))* by Lisa Bullard
- *Alligators (Blastoff! Readers: Animal Safari)* by Derek Zobel
- *Look Out for Turtles! (Let's-Read-and-Find... Science 2)* by Melvin Berger
- *Endangered Sea Turtles (Earth's Endangered Animals)* by Bobbie Kalman
- *Turtle Splash!: Countdown at the Pond* by Cathryn Falwell
- *From Tadpole to Frog (Let's-Read-and-Find... Science 1)* by Wendy Pfeffer
- *Frogs and Toads and Tadpoles, Too (Rookie Read-About Science)* by Allan Fowler
- *National Geographic Readers: Frogs!* by Elizabeth Carney

Animals Week 17

- *What's It Like to Be a Fish? (Let's-Read-and-Find... Science 1)* by Wendy Pfeffer
- *Where Fish Go In Winter* by Amy Goldman Koss and Laura J. Bryant
- *The Life Cycle of Fish (Life Cycles)* by Darlene R. Stille
- *Sea Horse (Life Cycle of A...)* by Bobbie Kalman
- *Project Seahorse (Scientists in the Field Series)* by Pamela S. Turner
- *Mister Seahorse* by Eric Carle
- *Face to Face With Sharks (Face to Face with Animals)* by David Doubilet
- *Shark (Life Cycle of A...)* by John Crossingham
- *National Geographic Readers: Sharks! (Science Reader Level 2)* by Anne Schreiber

Animals Week 18

- *Wiggling Worms at Work (Let's-Read-and-Find... Science 2)* by Wendy Pfeffer
- *Diary of a Worm* by Doreen Cronin
- *Worms (First Step Nonfiction)* by Robin Nelson
- *Are You a Snail? (Backyard Books)* by Judy Allen
- *Life of the Snail (Nature Watch)* by Theres Buholzer
- *Tiny Snail* by Tammy Carter Bronson

- *An Octopus Is Amazing (Let's-Read-and-Find... Science, Stage 2)* by Patricia Lauber
- *Octopus (Day in the Life: Sea Animals)* by Louise Spilsbury
- *Good Thing You're Not an Octopus!* by Julie Markes and Maggie Smith

Animals Week 19

- *Shrimp (Blastoff! Readers: Oceans Alive)* by Colleen A. Sexton
- *Shrimp (Underwater World)* by Deborah Coldiron
- *A Day on a Shrimp Boat* by Ching Yeung Russell
- *Crab (Welcome Books: Ocean Life)* by Lloyd G. Douglas
- *In One Tidepool: Crabs, Snails, and Salty Tails* by Anthony D. Fredericks
- *Clumsy Crab* by Ruth Galloway
- *Time For Kids: Spiders!*
- *Spinning Spiders (Let's-Read-and-Find... Science 2)* by Melvin Berger
- *The Very Busy Spider* by Eric Carle
- *Diary of a Spider* by Doreen Cronin

Animals Week 20

- *Ant Cities (Let's-Read-and-Find... Science 2)* by Arthur Dorros
- *National Geographic Readers: Ants* by Melissa Stewart
- *Are You an Ant? (Backyard Books)* by Judy Allen
- *From Caterpillar to Butterfly (Let's-Read-and-Find...)* by Deborah Heiligman
- *National Geographic Readers: Great Migrations Butterflies* by Laura F. Marsh
- *Caterpillars and Butterflies (Usborne Beginners)* by Stephanie Turnbull
- *Life of a Grasshopper (Life Cycles (Raintree Paperback))* by Clare Hibbert
- *Grasshoppers (Bugs Bugs Bugs)* by Margaret Hall
- *Are You a Grasshopper? (Backyard Books)* by Judy Allen

Human Body Unit

Human Body Week 1

- *BodyWorks - Skin and Hair* by Katherine Goode
- *Your Skin and Mine: Revised Edition (Let's-Read-and-Find... Science 2)* by Paul Showers

Human Body Week 2

- *The Skeleton Inside You (Let's-Read-and-Find... Science 2)* by Philip Balestrino
- *Bones: Skeletons and How They Work* by Steve Jenkins
- *A Book about Your Skeleton (Hello Reader!)* by Ruth Belov Gross

Human Body Week 3

- *Bend and Stretch: Learning About Your Bones and Muscles (Amazing Body)* by Pamela Hill Nettleton
- *The Mighty Muscular-Skeletal System: How Do My Bones and Muscles Work?* by John Burstein
- *Your Muscles (Your Body)* by Anne Ylvisaker

Human Body Week 4

- *The Nervous System (New True Books: Health)* by Christine Taylor-Butler
- *The Brain: Our Nervous System* by Seymour Simon
- *Brain, Nerves, and Senses (Understanding the Human Body)* by Steve Parker
- *You've Got Nerve!: The Secrets of the Brain and Nerves (The Gross and Goofy Body)* by Melissa Stewart

Human Body Week 5

- *Look, Listen, Taste, Touch, and Smell: Learning About Your Five Senses (Amazing Body)* by Pamela Hill Nettleton
- *My Five Senses Big Book (Let's-Read-And-Find...* by Margaret Miller and Aliki
- *The Magic School Bus Explores the Senses* by Joanna Cole
- *The Listening Walk* by Paul Showers

Human Body Week 6

- *The Heart: Our Circulatory System* by Seymour Simon
- *The Circulatory Story* by Mary K. Corcoran
- *The Amazing Circulatory System: How Does My Heart Work?* by John Burstein
- *Hear Your Heart (Let's-Read-and-Find... Science 2)* by Paul Showers and Holly Keller
- *The Magic School Bus Has a Heart* by Anne Capeci and Carolyn Bracken

Human Body Week 7

- *The Respiratory System: Why Do I Feel Out of Breath?* by Sue Barraclough
- *How Do Your Lungs Work? (Rookie Read-About Health)* by Don L. Curry
- *The Remarkable Respiratory System: How Do My Lungs Work?* by John Burstein
- *Breathe In, Breathe Out: Learning About Your Lungs (Amazing Body)* by Pamela Hill Nettleton

Human Body Week 8

- *What Happens to a Hamburger? (Let's-Read-and-Find... Science 2)* by Paul Showers
- *Where Does Your Food Go? (Rookie Read-About Health)* by Wiley Blevins
- *The Dynamic Digestive System: How Does My Stomach Work?* by John Burstein
- *Guts: Our Digestive System* by Seymour Simon

Human Body Week 9

- *The Digestive and Excretory Systems (The Human Body Library)* by Susan Dudley Gold
- *Learning about the Digestive and Excretory Systems (Learning about the Human Body Systems)* by Susan Dudley Gold
- *My Messy Body (Body Works)* by Liza Fromer, Francine and Joe Weissmann
- *Have a Nice DNA (Enjoy Your Cells, 3)* by Fran Balkwill and Mic Rolph

Human Body Week 10

- *The Immune System Your Magic Doctor: A Guide to the Immune System for the Curious of All Ages* by Helen Garvy and Dan Bessie
- *Body Warriors: The Immune System* by Lisa Trumbauer
- *Our Immune System (Our Bodies (Discovery Library))* by Susan Thames

- *Germs* by Ross Collins

Plants

Plants Week 1

- *Why Do Leaves Change Color? (Let's-Read-and-Find... Science, Stage 2)* by Betsy Maestro
- *Leaves (Designs for Coloring)* by Ruth Heller
- *Leaf Jumpers* by Carole Gerber
- *Leaves* by David Ezra Stein
- *Photosynthesis: Changing Sunlight Into Food (Nature's Changes)* by Bobbie Kalman

Plants Week 2

- *The Reason for a Flower (World of Nature)* by Ruth Heller
- *A Weed Is a Flower* by Aliki
- *Flower (Life Cycle of A…)* by Molly Aloian

Plants Week 3

- *Seeds* by Ken Robbins
- *From Seed to Plant* by Gail Gibbons
- *A Fruit Is a Suitcase for Seeds* by Jean Richards
- *From Seed to Apple (How Living Things Grow)* by Anita Ganeri
- *How a Seed Grows (Let's-Read-and-Find... Science 1)* by Helene J. Jordan
- *The Tiny Seed (World of Eric Carle)* by Eric Carle

Plants Week 4

- *Plants That Never Ever Bloom (Explore!)* by Ruth Heller
- *Ferns (Rookie Read-About Science)* by Allan Fowler
- *From Pine cone to Pine Tree* by Ellen Weiss
- *Fungi: Mushrooms, Toadstools, Molds, Yeasts, and Other Fungi* by Judy Wearing
- *Fungi (Kid's Guide to the Classification of Living Things)* by Elaine Pascoe and Janet Powell

Plants Week 5

- *Stems (Plant Parts)* by Vijaya Bodach
- *Plant Plumbing: A Book About Roots and Stems* by Susan Blackaby
- *Stems (World of Plants)* by John Farndon
- *Plant Cells and Life Processes (Investigating Cells)* by Barbara A. Somerville
- *Powerful Plant Cells (Microquests)* by Rebecca L Johnson and Jack Desrocher

Plants Week 6

- *What Do Roots Do?* by Kathleen V. Kudlinski
- *Roots (Plant Parts series)* by Vijaya Bodach

Supplies Needed by Week

Animals Unit

Week	Supplies needed
1	Shoe-box, Construction paper, Glue, Markers
2	Newspaper, Plain paper, Black and green construction paper
3	2 Toilet paper tubes, Piece of foil, Piece of black construction paper, 2 Rubber bands, Flashlight
4	A pack of colored pipe cleaners, 4 Wooden stakes (or pencils), String (about 80 ft.), Ruler
5	4x4 Piece of cardboard, 1 Cup sand or salt, Dime, Large jar lid
6	2 Small cans, Washcloth, Rubber band
7	Paper cups, Ticking watch, Ruler
8	Two thermometers, 2 Glasses, One large bowl
9	Rubber bands
10	2 Glass jars, Box at least 2 inches wider and taller than the jars, Cotton balls, 2 Thermometers
11	Plastic soda bottle, Wood dowel, Seeds
12	1 Clear glass bowl, Measuring cup, Liquid oil, Powdered detergent, Measuring spoon
13	Scissors, Notebook paper, Ruler
14	1 Raw egg, 1 Jar with lid, White vinegar, Measuring tape
15	2 Thermometers, Trowel, White towel
16	No supplies needed.
17	Salt, Measuring spoon, 2 Shallow bowls, 1 Small cucumber, Masking tape, Marker
18	Suction cup, Rock
19	String
20	Paper clip, Printout from Science Around the World, Paint for butterfly, Construction paper

Human Body Unit

Week	Supplies needed
1	Typing paper, Pencil, Clear tape, Magnifying glass

Week	Supplies needed
2	1 Raw chicken bone, 1 Jar with lid, White vinegar
3	Items of various weights, such as a paper clip, toothbrush, glass, a can, a book
4	A large book or something else that will make a loud noise, Cotton balls (or rolled-up paper towels), See-through barrier (a wire screen, plastic or glass window)
5	Mirror, Toothpicks, Blindfold, Clothespin, Apple, Onion, Pencils, Masking tape
6	Modeling clay, Paper, Match
7	Plastic dishpan, 2 Feet of aquarium tubing, 1 Gallon milk jug, Masking tape, Pens
8	Paper towels, Slender glass jar, Masking tape, Marking pen
9	Family pictures
10	Milk, Measuring cup, 2 Pint Jars

Plants Unit

Week	Supplies needed
1	Alcohol, Green leaf, Coffee filter, Pencil, Baby food jar, Ruler
2	Measuring cup, 2 Glasses, 1 White carnation with long stem, Red and blue food coloring
3	10 or 12 Dry pinto beans, Jar, Paper towels
4	Pine cone (tightly closed), Magnifying glass
5	1 Glass, A piece of wilted celery, Blue food coloring
6	Paper towels, 4 Pinto beans, Masking tape, Drinking glass, Marking pen

Biology for the Grammar Stage

Animals Unit

Animals Unit Overview

(20 weeks)

Books Scheduled

Encyclopedias

- *Kingfisher First Encyclopedia of Animals*

  OR

- *DK Encyclopedia of Animals*

Scientific Demonstration Books

- *Janice VanCleave's Biology for Every Kid*
- *Janice VanCleave's Science Around the World*

Sequence for Study

- **Week 1:** Habitats and Animal Behavior, part 1 (Desert, Grasslands, Rainforest, Animal Diet)
- **Week 2:** Habitats and Animal Behavior part 2 (Woodlands, Arctic, Camouflage)
- **Week 3:** Mammals (Lion, Cheetah, Elephant)
- **Week 4:** Mammals, part 2 (Zebra, Hippo, Fox)
- **Week 5:** Mammals, part 3 (Giraffe, Camel, Deer)
- **Week 6:** Mammals, part 4 (Panda, Polar Bear, Chimpanzee)
- **Week 7:** Mammals, part 5 (Kangaroo, Koala, Beaver)
- **Week 8:** Mammals, part 6 (Armadillo, Skunk, Rabbit)
- **Week 9:** Mammals, part 7 (Walrus, Whale, Dolphin)
- **Week 10:** Mammals, part 8 (Goat, Cow, Pig)
- **Week 11:** Birds, part 1 (Eagle, Owl, Parrot)
- **Week 12:** Birds, part 2 (Penguin, Chicken, Duck)
- **Week 13:** Birds, part 3 (Swan, Swallow, Hummingbird)
- **Week 14:** Birds, part 4 (Flamingo, Peacock, Ostrich)
- **Week 15:** Reptiles and Amphibians, part 1 (Chameleon, Iguana, Rattlesnake)
- **Week 16:** Reptiles and Amphibians, part 2 (Alligator, Turtle, Frog)
- **Week 17:** Fish (Salmon, Seahorse, Shark)
- **Week 18:** Invertebrates, part 1 (Worm, Snail, Octopus)
- **Week 19:** Invertebrates, part 2 (Shrimp, Crab, Spider)
- **Week 20:** Invertebrates, part 3 (Ant, Butterfly, Grasshopper)

Animal Poems to Memorize

<u>Characteristics of Mammals</u>

Mammals love to breathe air
They all have fur or hair
Their blood is warm, almost hot
Their babies drink milk a lot!

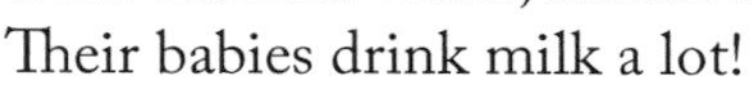

Characteristics of Birds
Birds have wings
Most like to sing
They make beautiful nests
Where they lay eggs and rest

Characteristics of Reptiles
Reptiles like meat
Their blood is cold - sweet!
They have scaly, watertight skin
And in their nests their eggs lay in

Characteristics of Amphibians
Amphibians can live on water or land
They lay eggs and have cold blood - grand!

Characteristics of Fish
Fish swim in the sea with the otter
Using their gills to breathe in the water
They lay eggs that float through the ocean
And their strong skeletons keep them in motion

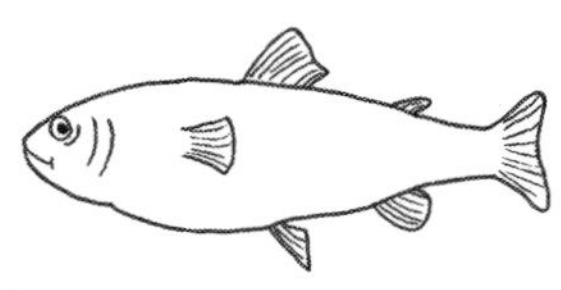

Characteristics of Invertebrates
Invertebrates have no backbone
They live worldwide, in every zone
Ninety-seven percent of animals are in this group
Like the clams and shrimp that end up in your soup

Supplies Needed for the Unit

Week	Supplies needed
1	Shoe-box, Construction paper, Glue, Markers
2	Newspaper, Plain paper, Black and green construction paper
3	2 Toilet paper tubes, Piece of foil, Piece of black construction paper, 2 Rubber bands, Flashlight
4	A pack of colored pipe cleaners, 4 Wooden stakes (or pencils), String (about 80 ft.), Ruler
5	4x4 Piece of cardboard, 1 Cup sand or salt, Dime, Large jar lid

Week	Supplies needed
6	2 Small cans, Washcloth, Rubber band
7	Paper cups, Ticking watch, Ruler
8	Two thermometers, 2 Glasses, One large bowl
9	Rubber bands
10	2 Glass jars, Box at least 2 inches wider and taller than the jars, Cotton balls, 2 Thermometers
11	Plastic soda bottle, Wood dowel, Seeds
12	1 Clear glass bowl, Measuring cup, Liquid oil, Powdered detergent, Measuring spoon
13	Scissors, Notebook paper, Ruler
14	1 Raw egg, 1 Jar with lid, White vinegar, Measuring tape
15	2 Thermometers, Trowel, White towel
16	**No supplies needed.**
17	Salt, Measuring spoon, 2 Shallow bowls, 1 Small cucumber, Masking tape, Marker
18	Suction cup, Rock
19	String
20	Paper clip, Printout from Science Around the World, Paint for butterfly, Construction paper

Unit Vocabulary

1. **Herbivore –** An animal that feeds on plants.
2. **Carnivore –** An animal that feeds on other animals.
3. **Omnivore –** An animal that feeds both on plants and animals.
4. **Habitat –** The natural environment of a plant or animal; a place that is natural for the life and growth of an animal or plant.
5. **Mammals –** Any warm-blooded vertebrate with skin that is more or less covered with hair; they give birth to live young that are nourished with milk at the beginning of their life.
6. **Wild Animal –** An animal that is typically found only in the wild.
7. **Vertebrate –** An animal with a backbone.
8. **Marine Mammal –** An animal that has all the characteristics of a mammal, but that also lives in the water.
9. **Domesticated Animal –** An animal that has been under human control for many generations.
10. **Bird –** A warm-blooded, egg-laying, feathered vertebrate; it also has wings.

11. **Migration** – A journey made by an animal to a new habitat.
12. **Egg** – The reproductive structure of some animals.
13. **Reptile** – A group of cold-blooded animals that usually have rough skin.
14. **Amphibian** – A cold-blooded, smooth-skinned vertebrate, such as a frog or salamander.
15. **Fish** – A cold-blooded, aquatic vertebrate with gills and fins; it typically also has an elongated body covered with scales.
16. **Invertebrate** – An animal without a backbone.
17. **Shellfish** – An aquatic invertebrate animal with a shell.
18. **Insect** – An invertebrate animal that has three body parts (head, thorax, and abdomen) and six legs.

Week 1: Habitats and Animal Behavior, Part 1 Lesson Plans

Scientific Demonstration: Habitat Diorama

Supplies Needed

- ✓ Shoe-box
- ✓ Construction paper
- ✓ Glue
- ✓ Markers

Purpose

This demonstration is meant to give the students a first hand look at their chosen habitat.

Instructions

1. Have the students choose which habitat they would like to create.
2. Then, have them create that environment inside of a shoe-box using construction paper and markers. (**Note** — *If you would like to add animals to the students' habitats, they can use the small animal pictures on SW pp. 107 and 109. I have also included a placement guide for these animals in the Appendix on pg. 179 of this guide.*)
3. Have the students dictate, copy, or write one to four sentences on their finished habitat diorama on SW pg. 9.

Take it Further

Instead of making a habitat diorama, make a poster depicting one or more habitats. You could make one large poster with several habitats or several smaller ones, each with one habitat. I have included several single sheet habitats in the Appendix on pp. 180-186 of this guide that you can copy for personal use.

Science-Oriented Books

Reading Assignments

- *Kingfisher Encyclopedia of Animals pg. 12 (Food)* [**Note** — *You will need to read about the desert, grasslands, and rainforest habitats from one of the additional suggested books or from Janice VanCleave's Science Around the World pp. 70–71, 84–85 (Desert), pp. 49–50, 60–61 (Grassland), and pp. 5–6 (Rainforest)*]
- *DK Encyclopedia of Animals pp. 68–69 (Deserts), pp. 64–65 (Grasslands) pp. 60–61 (Rainforest), pp. 30–33 (Plant-Eaters and Meat-Eaters)*

(Optional) Additional topic to explore this week: Communication

Discussion Questions

After reading the selected pages from the encyclopedias, ask the following questions in your discussion time:

Habitats (*Ask these questions for each habitat.*)

? What does the habitat look like?

- ? How much rain does it get?
- ? What is the average temperature in the habitat?

Animal Diet (Note — *There is no narration sheet for this topic.)*

- ? What kinds of foods do carnivores eat? Herbivores? Omnivores?

(Optional) Additional Books

- *A Desert Habitat (Introducing Habitats)* by Kelley Macaulay and Bobbie Kalman
- *About Habitats: Deserts* by Cathryn P. Sill
- *Life in the Desert (Pebble Plus: Habitats Around the World)* by Alison Auch
- *A Grassland Habitat (Introducing Habitats)* by Kelley Macaulay and Bobbie Kalman
- *Grasslands (About Habitats)* by Cathryn P. Sill
- *A Savanna Habitat (Introducing Habitats)* by Bobbie Kalman
- *A Rainforest Habitat (Introducing Habitats)* by Molly Aloian

Notebooking

Writing Assignments

- **Narration Page** – Have the students dictate, copy, or write one to four sentences for each of the habitats on SW pg. 8. They can include information on the amount of rainfall, the typical temperature, and the main characteristics of the habitat. For example, for this week the student could dictate, copy, or write the following for the grassland habitat:

  The grasslands have an average amount of rain.
  It can have hot summers and cooler winters.
  The grasslands have lots of grass, very few trees, and lots of animals.

- **(Optional) Lapbook** – Complete the Desert and Grassland Habitat Tab-book on pp. 7-10 from *Biology for the Grammar Stage Lapbooking Templates*. For each one, cut out the pages and color the cover. Then, have the students color on the map where the desert habitat is typically found on the "Locations" page. After that, have the students tell you what they have learned about the desert and write it for them on the "Characteristics" page. Next, have them color the animals that can be found in the habitat and label them on the "Animals" page. Lastly, staple the pages together and glue the habitat tab books into the lapbook.

Vocabulary

The following definitions are a guide. The students' definitions do not need to match word for word.

- **Herbivore** – An animal that feeds on plants. (SW pg. 93)
- **Carnivore** – An animal that feeds on other animals. (SW pg. 91)
- **Omnivore** – An animal that feeds both on plants and animals. (SW pg. 96)

Multi-week Projects and Activities

Unit Project

- **Animal Diet Chart –** The Animal Diet Chart project will continue throughout this unit. For this week, have the students write down what the animals in each of the three categories (herbivore, omnivore, and carnivore) prefer to eat on SW pp. 6-7. Once the students begin to study the different animals, they will add each one to the chart as they learn about it. I have included a placement chart for this project on pg. 178.

Projects for this Week

- **Coloring Pages –** You can have the students color the following pages from *Biology for the Grammar Stage Coloring Pages*: Desert pg. 7, Grasslands pg. 8, Rainforest pg. 9.
- **Animal Diet –** Have the students make the food mobile shown on page 12 of *Kingfisher First Encyclopedia of Animals.*
- **Rainforest –** Have the students make a rainforest in a bottle. Please visit the following website for directions on this project:
  - http://earthobservatory.nasa.gov/Experiments/Biome/hobuildrainforest.php

Memorization

- There is nothing to memorize this week.

Quiz

Weekly Quiz

- "Animals Unit Week 1 Quiz" on SW pg. Q-5.

Quiz Answers

1. Herbivore — eats only plants; Carnivore — eats only meat; Omnivore — eats both plants and meat.
2. Grassland — grass is the main plant; Desert — typically very hot and dry; Rainforest — has lots of rain.
3. Answers will vary

Notes

Possible Schedules for Week 1

Two Days a Week Schedule	
Day 1	**Day 2**
❑ Read about the Desert, Grasslands, and Rainforest ❑ Complete the Narration Page for this week ❑ Work on the Habitat Diorama Project	❑ Read about Food (or Plant-eaters and Meat-eaters) ❑ Add information to the Animal Diet Chart ❑ Define herbivore, carnivore, and omnivore ❑ Take the Animal Week 1 quiz

Five Days a Week Schedule				
Day 1	**Day 2**	**Day 3**	**Day 4**	**Day 5**
❑ Read about the Desert and Grasslands ❑ Add information on the Desert and Grasslands to the Narration Page	❑ Read about the Rainforest ❑ Complete the Narration Page for this week ❑ Do the Rainforest Project	❑ Read about Food (or Plant-eaters and Meat-eaters) ❑ Add information to the Animal Diet Chart ❑ Do the Animal Diet project	❑ Work on the Habitat Diorama Project ❑ Define herbivore, carnivore, and omnivore	❑ Take the Animal Week 1 quiz

Week 2: Habitats & Animal Behavior, Part 2 Lesson Plans

Scientific Demonstration: Camouflage

Supplies Needed

- ✓ Newspaper
- ✓ Plain Paper
- ✓ Black and Green Construction Paper

Purpose

This demonstration is meant to help the students to see the benefit of camouflage and why animals use this method as a form of defense.

Instructions

1. Cut out several of the same shapes from each of the four types of paper, including the same newspaper that you will use in step 2.
2. Lay out a sheet of newspaper on the table and then lay the shapes on top of the paper.
3. Have the students come in and try to identify the number and types of shapes that are on the newspaper. (*The students should see that the newspaper blended the best, followed by the black construction paper, the white construction paper and the green construction paper.*)
4. Have the students complete the Lab Report on SW pg. 11.

Explanation

Your students noticed the green shapes first and the newspaper shapes last. This is because the newspaper is most like the background that it was on, while the green shapes are the most different. Animals use this same concept to hide themselves in their environment. In biology, we call this being camouflaged. The animal has similar colors to those found in its habitat, which can keep us from noticing it. It also helps the animal hide from predators, which increases its chance of survival.

Take it Further

Have the students move the shapes around; is there a better position or place that will camouflage the shapes more adequately? You can also have them design their own camouflage background for the green, black or white shapes.

Science-Oriented Books

Reading Assignments

- *Kingfisher Encyclopedia of Animals pg. 11 (Camouflage) [***Note:** *You will need to read about the forest and arctic habitats from one of the additional suggested books or from Janice VanCleave's Science Around the World pp. 22-23, 37-38 (Forest) and pp. 93-94, 106-107 (Arctic Tundra)]*
- *DK Encyclopedia of Animals pp. 36-37 (Camouflage), pp. 60-61 (Woodlands), pp. 54-55*

(Arctic), pp. 56–57 (Antarctic)

(Optional) Additional topic to explore this week: Defense

Discussion Questions

After reading the selected pages from the encyclopedias, ask the following questions in your discussion time:

Habitats (*Ask these questions for each habitat.*)

- ? What does the habitat look like?
- ? How much rain does it get?
- ? What is the average temperature in the habitat?

Camouflage

- ? In what ways do animals use camouflage?
- ? Why do animals use camouflage?

(Optional) Additional Books

- *A Forest Habitat (Introducing Habitats)* by Bobbie Kalman
- *Northern Refuge: A Story of a Canadian Boreal Forest* by Audrey Fraggalosch
- *The Arctic Habitat (Introducing Habitats)* by Molly Aloian and Bobbie Kalman
- *Arctic Tundra (Habitats)* by Michael H. Forman
- *Arctic Tundra* by Donald M. Silver

Notebooking

Writing Assignments

- ☐ **Narration Page –** Have the students dictate, copy, or write one to four sentences for each of the habitats on SW pg. 10. They can include information on the amount of rainfall, the typical temperature, and the main characteristics of the habitat. Also have them dictate, copy, or write one to four sentences for camouflage on SW pg. 10.
- ☐ **(Optional) Lapbook –** Complete the Forest and Arctic Habitat Tab Book on pp. 11-14 from *Biology for the Grammar Stage Lapbooking Templates*. For each one, cut out the pages and color the cover. Then, have the students color on the map where the desert habitat is typically found on the "Locations" page. After that, have the students tell you what they have learned about the desert and write it for them on the "Characteristics" page. Next, have them color the animals that can be found in the habitat and label them on the "Animals" page. Lastly, staple the pages together and glue the habitat tab books into the lapbook.

Vocabulary

The following definition is a guide; the students' definitions do not need to match word for word.

- **Habitat –** The natural environment of a plant or animal; a place that is natural for the life and growth of an animal or plant. (SW pg. 93)

Multi-week Projects and Activities

Unit Project

- ✂ **(Optional) Habitat Posters** – Have the students color the habitat posters found in the Appendix on pp. 180-186. Then, mount them on the wall or in a notebook. Over the next eighteen weeks, you will add animals to these habitat posters. You will need to make a copy of the pictures on SW pp. 107 and 109 for this project.

Projects for this Week

- ✂ **Coloring Pages** – You can have the students color the following pages from *Biology for the Grammar Stage Coloring Pages*: Woodlands pg. 10, Arctic pg. 11, Camouflage pg. 12.
- ✂ **Planet Earth DVD Series** – Watch the BBC Planet Earth series with the students. This series has stunning photography of the habitats around the world but it is also very realistic. It does not shy away from showing the natural predator/prey relationships. If you have sensitive children you may want to preview the movie to make sure that it won't scare them.

Memorization

There is nothing to memorize this week.

Quiz

Weekly Quiz

- "Animal Week 2 Quiz" on SW pg. Q-6.

Quiz Answers

1. True
2. Cold
3. True
4. Hide
5. Answers will vary

Notes

Possible Schedules for Week 2

Two Days a Week Schedule	
Day 1	**Day 2**
❑ Read about Camouflage ❑ Add information on camouflage to the Narration Page ❑ Do the Scientific Demonstration: Camouflage	❑ Read about the Woodlands, Arctic and Antarctica ❑ Complete the Narration Page for this week ❑ Finish working on the Habitat Diorama ❑ Define habitat ❑ Take the Animal Week 2 quiz

Five Days a Week Schedule				
Day 1	**Day 2**	**Day 3**	**Day 4**	**Day 5**
❑ Read about the Woodlands ❑ Add information on the Woodlands to the Narration Page ❑ Define habitat	❑ Read about the Arctic and Antarctic ❑ Add information on the Arctic to the Narration Page ❑ Watch part of the BBC Planet Earth Series	❑ Read about Camouflage ❑ Add information on camouflage to the Narration Page ❑ Watch part of the BBC Planet Earth Series	❑ Do the Scientific Demonstration: Camouflage ❑ Watch part of the BBC Planet Earth Series	❑ Take the Animal Week 2 quiz ❑ Watch part of the BBC Planet Earth Series

Week 3: Mammals, Part 1 Lesson Plans

Scientific Demonstration: Cat's Eyes

Supplies Needed

- ✓ Toilet paper tube
- ✓ Foil
- ✓ Rubber bands
- ✓ Construction paper
- ✓ Flashlight

Purpose

This demonstration is meant to help the students to see why a cat's eyes seem to glow in the night.

Instructions

1. Cover one end of one of the toilet paper tubes with the foil and cover the other with construction paper. Secure both with rubber bands.
2. Take your tubes and your flashlight and go into a dark room.
3. Shine the flashlight into the tubes; what happens?
4. Have the students complete the Lab Report on SW pg. 13.

Explanation

The students should see that the tube with the foil on the bottom appears to shine. This is because the foil reflects light, just like a cat's eye. The back of a cat's eye contains a substance that can reflect light, which makes the eyes appear to glow in the dark.

Take it Further

See what happens to the students' pupils in the presence of light by going into a dark room and turning on the lights. Have them watch each others' eyes to see what happens.

Science-Oriented Books

Reading Assignments

- *Kingfisher Encyclopedia of Animals pg. 20 (Mammal), pg. 21 (Lion), pg. 24 (Cheetah), pg. 26 (Elephant)*
- *DK Encyclopedia of Animals pp. 239-241 (Mammal), pp. 231-233 (Lion), pp. 136-137 (Cheetah), pp. 170-172 (Elephant)*

(Optional) Coordinating animals to study this week: Leopard, Puma, Tiger

Discussion Questions

After reading the selected pages from the encyclopedias, ask the following questions for each of the animals in your discussion time:

- ? What are two things you learned about ________?
- ? What did you find interesting about ________?

- ? What kind of food does a ________ eat?
- ? Where do you usually find a ________?

(Optional) Additional Books

- *What is a Mammal? (Science of Living Things)* by Kalman
- *Face to Face with Lions (Face to Face with Animals)* by Beverly Joubert
- *Tawny Scrawny Lion (Little Golden Book)* by Golden Books and Gustaf Tenggren
- *The Cheetah: Fast as Lightning (Animal Close-Ups)* by Christine Denis-Huot and Michel Denis-Huot
- *Cheetah (Welcome Books: Animals of the World)* by Edana Eckart
- *Cheetah Cubs: Station Stop 2 (All Aboard Science Reader)* by Ginjer L. Clarke and Lucia Washburn
- *Elephants: A Book for Children* by Steve Bloom
- *Face to Face With Elephants (Face to Face with Animals)* by Beverly Joubert

Notebooking

Writing Assignments

- **Narration Page –** Have the students dictate, copy, or write one to four sentences for each animal on SW pg. 12. You can also have them record what habitat the animal typically lives in and whether the animal is a herbivore, omnivore, or carnivore. For example, for this week the student could dictate, copy, or write the following for the lion:

  The male lion roars to scare off people.
  The female lion hunts and takes care of the babies.
  Diet: Carnivore
  Habitat: Grasslands

- **(Optional) Lapbook –** Work on Animals #1 Flap-book on pg. 18 from *Biology for the Grammar Stage Lapbooking Templates*. Color the lion, cheetah, and elephant pictures on the flap-book. Have the students tell you what they have learned about the animals. Then, write for them their favorite piece of information on the inside of the flap-book for each animal.

Vocabulary

The following definition is a guide; the students' definitions do not need to match word for word.

- **Mammals –** Any warm-blooded vertebrate with skin that is more or less covered with hair; they give birth to live young that are nourished with milk at the beginning of their life. (SW pg. 95)

Multi-week Projects and Activities

Unit Project

- **Animal Diet Chart –** Add the lion, cheetah, and elephant to the Animal Diet Chart on SW pp. 6-7; pictures for this project are on SW pg. 107. The placement chart for this project can be found in the Appendix on pg. 178.

✂ **(Optional) Habitat Posters** – This week, add the lion, cheetah, and elephant to the habitat posters that the students colored last week. The placement chart for this project can be found in the Appendix on pg. 179.

Projects for this Week

✂ **Coloring Pages** – You can have the students color the following pages from *Biology for the Grammar Stage Coloring Pages*: Lion pg. 13, Cheetah pg. 14, Elephant pg. 15.

✂ **Lion** – Have the students make a lion out of an egg carton! You will need an egg carton, tissue paper, paint, wiggly eyes, and glue. Simply follow the directions from the following website:

http://onecrayolashort.blogspot.com/2010/03/egg-carton-lions.html

✂ **Cheetah** – Have the students make a cheetah mask. You will need a paper plate and pom-poms, along with yellow and brown point. Begin by painting a paper plate completely yellow. Then, dip a pom-pom into brown paint and use it to add spots to the plate. Cut out holes for the eyes and add two yellow triangles for ears. Finally, add a string so that the students can wear their mask.

✂ **Elephant** – Have the students make their own elephant trunk. You will need a grey sock, stuffing, and an elastic band. Begin by using a grey sock and stuffing it with paper or cotton to give it more stability. Next, staple an elastic band on either side of the sock, so that the sock will fit around your head. Then, sit your trunk in front of your nose and pretend to be an elephant.

Memorization

This week, begin to work on memorizing the *Characteristics of Mammals* poem. (SW pg. 100)

Characteristics of Mammals
Mammals love to breathe air
They all have fur or hair
Their blood is warm, almost hot
Their babies drink milk a lot!

Quiz

Weekly Quiz

- "Animal Week 3 Quiz" on SW pg. Q-7

Quiz Answers

1. False (*Cheetahs are the fastest mammals on Earth.*)
2. Heaviest
3. True
4. Warm-blooded, hairy, babies drink milk
5. Answers will vary

Possible Schedules for Week 3

Two Days a Week Schedule	
Day 1	**Day 2**
❑ Read about Mammals and the Lion ❑ Add information about the lion to the students' Narration Page ❑ Do the Scientific Demonstration: Cat's Eyes ❑ Define mammal ❑ Work on memorizing the *Characteristics of Mammals* Poem	❑ Read about the Cheetah and Elephant ❑ Complete the students' Narration Page ❑ Add this week's animals to the Animal Diet Chart (or the Habitat Posters) ❑ Take the Animal Week 3 quiz ❑ Choose one of the projects from the week to complete

Five Days a Week Schedule				
Day 1	**Day 2**	**Day 3**	**Day 4**	**Day 5**
❑ Read about the Lion ❑ Add information about the lion to the students' Narration Page ❑ Do the Lion Project	❑ Read about Mammals ❑ Do the Scientific Demonstration: Cat's Eyes ❑ Define mammal	❑ Read about the Cheetah ❑ Add information about the cheetah to the students' Narration Page ❑ Do the Cheetah Project	❑ Read about the Elephant ❑ Add information about the elephant to the students' Narration Page ❑ Do the Elephant Project	❑ Take the Animal Week 3 quiz ❑ Add this week's animals to the Animal Diet Chart (or the Habitat Posters)
All Week Long ❑ Work on memorizing the *Characteristics of Mammals* Poem				

Notes

Week 4: Mammals, Part 2 Lesson Plans

Scientific Demonstration: Blending

Supplies Needed

- ✓ A pack of colored pipe cleaners
- ✓ 4 Wooden stakes (or pencils)
- ✓ String (about 80 ft.)
- ✓ Ruler

Purpose

This demonstration is meant to help the students to see how animals can use their color to blend into their environment or to blend together, both of which help to protect them against predators.

Instructions and Explanation

The instructions and explanation for this scientific demonstration are found on pp. 128-129 of *Janice VanCleave's Biology for Every Kid*. Have the students complete the Lab Report on SW pg. 15.

Take it Further

Have the students learn more about how a herd of zebras use stripes to blend together and protect themselves against predators. Check out the video below for a brief explanation:

- http://kids.nationalgeographic.com/kids/animals/creaturefeature/zebra/ (*Please preview this website before allowing the students to watch the video to make sure it is appropriate for your group.*)

Science-Oriented Books

Reading Assignments

- *Kingfisher Encyclopedia of Animals pg. 27 (Zebra), pg.29 (Hippopotamus), pg. 33 (Fox)*
- *DK Encyclopedia of Animals pp. 361-363 (Zebra), pp. 201-203 (Hippopotamus), pp. 179-180 (Fox)*

(Optional) Coordinating animals to study this week: Donkey, Horse, Dog (wild), Dog (domestic), Wolf

Discussion Questions

After reading the selected pages from the encyclopedias, ask the following questions for each of the animals in your discussion time:

- ? What are two things you learned about ________?
- ? What did you find interesting about ________?
- ? What kind of food does a ________ eat?
- ? Where do you usually find a ________?

(Optional) Additional Books

- *Zebras (Wild Ones)* by Jill Anderson
- *How the Zebra Got Its Stripes (Little Golden Book)* by Justine Fontes
- *Hippos (Naturebooks: Safari Animals)* by Jenny Markert
- *The Hiccupotamus* by Aaron Zenz
- *Fox* by Kate Banks
- *Foxes (Animal Predators)* by Sandra Markle

Notebooking

Writing Assignments

- **Narration Page** – Have the students dictate, copy, or write one to four sentences for each animal on SW pg. 14. You can also have them record what habitat the animal typically lives in and whether the animal is a herbivore, omnivore, or carnivore. (*See Animals Week 3 Lesson Plans for an example.*)

- **(Optional) Lapbook** – Complete Animals #1 Flap-book on pg. 18 from *Biology for the Grammar Stage Lapbooking Templates.* Color the zebra, hippo, and fox pictures on the flap-book. Have the students tell you what they have learned about the animals. Then, write for them their favorite piece of information on the inside of the flap-book for each animal. Finally, glue the flap-book into the lapbook.

Vocabulary

There is no vocabulary for this week.

Multi-week Projects and Activities

Unit Project

- **Animal Diet Chart** – Add the zebra, hippo, and fox to the Animal Diet Chart on SW pp. 6-7; pictures for this project are on SW pg. 107. The placement chart for this project can be found in the Appendix on pg. 178.
- **(Optional) Habitat Posters** – This week, add the zebra, hippo, and fox to the students' habitat posters. The placement chart for this project can be found in the Appendix on pg. 179.

Projects for this Week

- **Coloring Pages** – You can have the students color the following pages from *Biology for the Grammar Stage Coloring Pages*: Zebra pg. 16, Hippo pg. 17, Fox pg. 18.
- **Zebra** – Have the students make a zebra out of shapes. Begin by cutting out one large oval, one large rectangular, and two small triangular shapes from a white sheet of paper. Place the rectangle at an angle and glue the oval to the top end for the zebra's head and neck. Then, glue the two

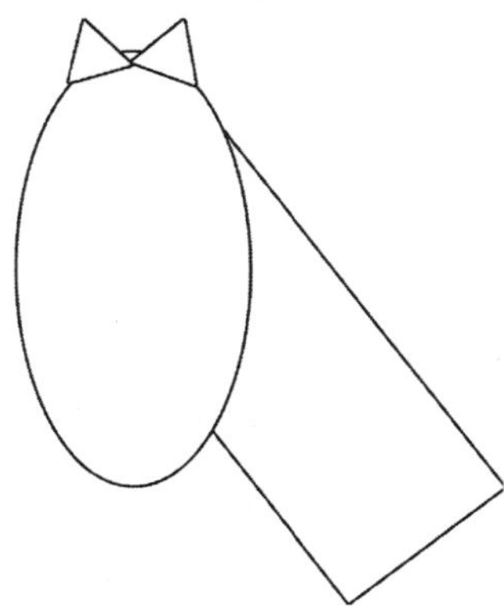

triangles at the top of the oval for the zebra's ears. Next, use black paint to give the zebra a nose, eyes and stripes. You can paint on the zebra's mane or glue a piece of black felt along the side of the rectangle instead. (**Note** — *If you do this project with an older student have them draw more realistically proportioned shapes.*)

- ✂ **Hippo –** Have the students make a Hippo Puzzle using the following website for directions:
  - http://www.zoosociety.org/Education/FunStuff/Hippo/

  (**Note** — *The website includes puzzle ideas for several different age groups.*)
- ✂ **Fox –** Many different types of foxes are endangered animals. Explain to the students what that means by saying, "Many different types of foxes are endangered animals, which means that there are not many of them left living in the wild. It also means that if we are not careful, the animals could die out and we would never see them again." If you know of an endangered species in your area, share that with the students. If not, look at this website to find endangered species that might live in your area.
  - http://www.earthsendangered.com/list.asp

  Try to learn a few facts about the animals and what the current conservation efforts are in your area.

Memorization

- Continue to work on memorizing the *Characteristics of Mammals* poem. (SW pg. 100)

Characteristics of Mammals
Mammals love to breathe air
They all have fur or hair
Their blood is warm, almost hot
Their babies drink milk a lot!

Quiz

Weekly Quiz

- "Animal Week 4 Quiz" on SW pg. Q-8.

Quiz Answers

1. False (*Every zebra has its own unique stripe pattern.*)
2. All of the above
3. True
4. Answers will vary

Notes

Possible Schedules for Week 4

Two Days a Week Schedule	
Day 1	**Day 2**
❑ Read about the Zebra ❑ Add information about the zebra to the students' Narration Page ❑ Do the Scientific Demonstration: Blending ❑ Work on memorizing the *Characteristics of Mammals* Poem	❑ Read about the Hippo and Fox ❑ Complete the students' Narration Page ❑ Add this week's animals to the Animal Diet Chart (or the Habitat Posters) ❑ Take the Animal Week 4 quiz ❑ Choose one of the projects from the week to complete

Five Days a Week Schedule				
Day 1	**Day 2**	**Day 3**	**Day 4**	**Day 5**
❑ Read about the Zebra ❑ Add information about the zebra to the students' Narration Page ❑ Do the Zebra Project	❑ Do the Scientific Demonstration: Blending	❑ Read about the Hippo ❑ Add information about the hippo to the students' Narration Page ❑ Do the Hippo Project	❑ Read about the Fox ❑ Add information about the fox to the students' Narration Page ❑ Do the Fox Project	❑ Take the Animal Week 4 quiz ❑ Add this week's animals to the Animal Diet Chart (or the Habitat Posters)
All Week Long ❑ Work on memorizing the *Characteristics of Mammals* Poem				

Week 5: Mammals, Part 3 Lesson Plans

Scientific Demonstration: Camels

Supplies Needed

- ✓ 4 x 4 Piece of cardboard
- ✓ 1 Cup sand or salt
- ✓ Dime
- ✓ Large jar lid

Purpose

This demonstration is meant to help the students to see the way camel's toes are designed to help them carry heavy loads across the soft desert sand.

Instructions and Explanation

The instructions and explanation for this scientific demonstration are found on pp. 82-83 of *Janice VanCleave's Science Around the World*. Have the students complete the Lab Report on SW pg. 17.

Take it Further

Do the additional demonstration described in *Janice VanCleave's Science Around the World* on pg. 83.

Science-Oriented Books

Reading Assignments

- *Kingfisher Encyclopedia of Animals pg. 34 (Giraffe), pg. 35 (Camel), pg. 38 (Deer)*
- *DK Encyclopedia of Animals pp. 187-189 (Giraffe), pp. 124-126 (Camel), pp. 154-156 (Deer)*

(Optional) Coordinating animals to study this week: Antelope, Buffalo, Llama, Elk, Reindeer

Discussion Questions

After reading the selected pages from the encyclopedias, ask the following questions for each of the animals in your discussion time:

- **?** What are two things you learned about ________?
- **?** What did you find interesting about ________?
- **?** What kind of food does a ________ eat?
- **?** Where do you usually find a ________?

(Optional) Additional Books

- *Giraffes* by Jill Anderson
- *Baby Giraffes (It's Fun to Learn about Baby Animals)* by Bobbie Kalman
- *Chee-Lin: A Giraffe's Journey* by James Rumford

- *Camels (Nature Watch)* by Cherie Winner
- *I Wonder Why Camels Have Humps: And Other Questions About Animals* by Anita Ganeri
- *Deer (Animals That Live in the Forest)* by JoAnn Early Macken
- *Deer (Blastoff! Readers: Backyard Wildlife)* by Derek Zobel

Notebooking

Writing Assignments

- ☐ **Narration Page** – Have the students dictate, copy, or write one to four sentences for each animal on SW pg. 16. You can also have them record what habitat the animal typically lives in and whether the animal is a herbivore, omnivore, or carnivore. (*See Animals Week 3 Lesson Plans for an example.*)

- ☐ **(Optional) Lapbook** – Work on Animals #2 Flap-book on pg. 19 from *Biology for the Grammar Stage Lapbooking Templates*. Color the giraffe, camel, and deer pictures on the flap-book. Have the students tell you what they have learned about the animals. Then, write for them their favorite piece of information on the inside of the flap-book for each animal.

Vocabulary

There is no vocabulary for this week.

Multi-week Projects and Activities

Unit Project

- ✂ **Animal Diet Chart** – Add the giraffe, camel, and deer to the Animal Diet Chart on SW pp. 6-7; pictures for this project are on SW pg. 107. The placement chart for this project can be found in the Appendix on pg. 178.
- ✂ **(Optional) Habitat Posters** – This week, add the giraffe, camel, and deer to the students' habitat posters. The placement chart for this project can be found in the Appendix on pg. 179.

Projects for this Week

- ✂ **Coloring Pages** – You can have the students color the following pages from *Biology for the Grammar Stage Coloring Pages*: Giraffe pg. 19, Camel pg. 20, Deer pg. 21.
- ✂ **Giraffe** – Have the students make a clothespin giraffe by following the directions from this website:
  - http://www.busybeekidscrafts.com/Clothes-Pin-Giraffe.html
- ✂ **Camel** – Have the students make an egg carton camel. Have them paint three egg cups from an egg carton brown. Once they are dry, attach two brown pipe cleaners each to two of the egg cups for the legs of the camel. Then, attach the two egg cups together to create the camel's body. After that, attach one end of another brown pipe cleaner to the body and the other end to the final egg cup. Glue googly eyes on either side of the egg cup for the camel's head.

✂ **Deer –** Have the students make some reindeer cookies by using Nutter Butter cookies, pretzels, M&M's and some frosting. Break the pretzels in half and use the frosting to attach them at the top of the cookie. Then attach a red M&M with frosting for the nose and two brown M&M's for the eyes of the reindeer. Eat and enjoy!

Memorization

Continue to work on memorizing the *Characteristics of Mammals* poem. (SW pg. 100)

Characteristics of Mammals
Mammals love to breathe air
They all have fur or hair
Their blood is warm, almost hot
Their babies drink milk a lot!

Quiz

Weekly Quiz

- "Animal Week 5 Quiz" on SW pg. Q-9.

Quiz Answers

1. Tallest
2. True
3. Big, wide
4. Answers will vary

Notes

Possible Schedules for Week 5

Two Days a Week Schedule	
Day 1	**Day 2**
❑ Read about the Camel ❑ Add information about the camel to the students' Narration Page ❑ Do the Scientific Demonstration: Camels ❑ Work on memorizing the *Characteristics of Mammals* Poem	❑ Read about the Giraffe and Deer ❑ Complete the students' Narration Page ❑ Add this week's animals to the Animal Diet Chart (or the Habitat Posters) ❑ Take the Animal Week 5 quiz ❑ Choose one of the projects from the week to complete

Five Days a Week Schedule				
Day 1	**Day 2**	**Day 3**	**Day 4**	**Day 5**
❑ Read about the Giraffe ❑ Add information about the giraffe to the students' Narration Page ❑ Do the Giraffe Project	❑ Read about the Camel ❑ Add information about the camel to the students' Narration Page ❑ Do the Camel Project	❑ Do the Scientific Demonstration: Camels	❑ Read about the Deer ❑ Add information about the deer to the students' Narration Page ❑ Do the Deer Project	❑ Take the Animal Week 5 quiz ❑ Add this week's animals to the Animal Diet Chart (or the Habitat Posters)
All Week Long ❑ Work on memorizing the *Characteristics of Mammals* Poem				

Week 6: Mammals, Part 4 Lesson Plans

Scientific Demonstration: Polar Bears

Supplies Needed

- ✓ 2 Small cans
- ✓ Washcloth
- ✓ Rubber band

Purpose

This demonstration is meant to help the students to see how the fur on a polar bear's feet keeps them from slipping on the ice.

Instructions and Explanation

The instructions and explanation for this scientific demonstration are found on pp. 104-105 of *Janice VanCleave's Science Around the World*. Have the students complete the Lab Report on SW pg. 19.

Take it Further

Do the additional demonstration described in *Janice VanCleave's Science Around the World* on pg. 105.

Science-Oriented Books

Reading Assignments

- *Kingfisher Encyclopedia of Animals pg. 41 (Panda), pg. 42 (Polar Bear), pg. 45 (Chimpanzee)*
- *DK Encyclopedia of Animals pp. 270-272 (Panda), pp. 283-284 (Polar Bear), pp.139-141 (Chimpanzee)*

(Optional) Coordinating animals to study this week: Raccoon, Bear, Baboon, Gorilla, Lemur, Monkey, Orangutan

Discussion Questions

After reading the selected pages from the encyclopedias, ask the following questions for each of the animals in your discussion time:

- **?** What are two things you learned about ________?
- **?** What did you find interesting about ________?
- **?** What kind of food does a ________ eat?
- **?** Where do you usually find a ________?

(Optional) Additional Books

- *Pi-Shu the Little Panda* by John Butler
- *Endangered Pandas (Earth's Endangered Animals)* by John Crossingham
- *Tracks of a Panda* by Nick Dowson
- *Face to Face with Polar Bears (Face to Face with Animals)* by Norbert Rosing and Elizabeth

Carney

- *Polar Bears* by Mark Newman
- *Where Do Polar Bears Live? (Let's-Read-and-Find... Science 2)* by Sarah L. Thomson
- *The Chimpanzee Family Book (Animal Family Series)* by Jane Goodall
- *Endangered Chimpanzees (Earth's Endangered Animals)* by Bobbie Kalman

Notebooking

Writing Assignments

- **Narration Page** – Have the students dictate, copy, or write one to four sentences for each animal on SW pg. 18. You can also have them record what habitat the animal typically lives in and whether the animal is a herbivore, omnivore, or carnivore. (*See Animals Week 3 Lesson Plans for an example.*)
- **(Optional) Lapbook** – Complete Animals #2 Flap-book on pg. 19 from *Biology for the Grammar Stage Lapbooking Templates*. Color the panda, polar bear, and chimpanzee pictures on the flap-book. Have the students tell you what they have learned about the animals. Then, write for them their favorite piece of information on the inside of the flap-book for each animal. Finally, glue the flap-book into the lapbook.

Vocabulary

There is no vocabulary for this week.

Multi-week Projects and Activities

Unit Project

- **Animal Diet Chart** – Add the panda, polar bear, and chimpanzee to the Animal Diet Chart on SW pp. 6-7; pictures for this project are on SW pg. 107. The placement chart for this project can be found in the Appendix on pg. 178.
- **(Optional) Habitat Posters** – This week, add the panda, polar bear, and chimpanzee to the students' habitat posters. The placement chart for this project can be found in the Appendix on pg. 179.

Projects for this Week

- **Coloring Pages** – You can have the students color the following pages from *Biology for the Grammar Stage Coloring Pages*: Panda pg. 22, Polar Bear pg. 23, Chimpanzee pg. 24.
- **Panda** – Have the students make a felt panda face using one large white felt circle, two medium sized black felt circles, two small black felt circles, one black felt triangle and two googly eyes. Use the large white felt circle for the base of the panda face and glue the two medium black felt circles at the top for ears. Then, glue the two small black felt circles in the center top for the eyes of the panda. Next, glue the triangle just below the eyes for the nose. Use a black permanent marker to draw a smile on your panda face and then draw a line from the bottom of the nose to the center of the smile. Finally glue the two googly eyes onto the two small black felt circles. (**Note** — *If you do this project with*

an older student, have him sew on all the pieces as well as the lines for the mouth.)

- ✂ **Polar Bear –** Have the students draw an arctic scene, complete with polar bears. The level of detail for this project will depend on the age of your students. For younger students, instruct them to use white paint to almost cover a black or dark blue sheet of paper. Then, once it is dry, have them use a marker to draw their polar bears. For older students, have them use white pastels on a dark sheet to create a winter scene. After that, have them use a very light shade of yellow to draw a polar bear so that it stands out a bit from the background.
- ✂ **Chimpanzee –** Read aloud the following book to your students over the next few weeks:
    - *My Life with the Chimpanzees* by Jane Goodall

Memorization

- Continue to work on memorizing the *Characteristics of Mammals* poem. (SW pg. 100)

<u>Characteristics of Mammals</u>
Mammals love to breathe air
They all have fur or hair
Their blood is warm, almost hot
Their babies drink milk a lot!

Quiz

Weekly Quiz

- "Animal Week 6 Quiz" on SW pg. Q-10.

Quiz Answers

1. True
2. A lot
3. Arctic
4. Answers will vary

Notes

Possible Schedules for Week 6

Two Days a Week Schedule	
Day 1	**Day 2**
❑ Read about the Polar Bear ❑ Add information about the polar bear to the students' Narration Page ❑ Do the Scientific Demonstration: Polar Bears ❑ Work on memorizing the *Characteristics of Mammals* Poem	❑ Read about the Panda and Chimpanzee ❑ Complete the students' Narration Page ❑ Add this week's animals to the Animal Diet Chart (or the Habitat Posters) ❑ Take the Animal Week 6 quiz ❑ Choose one of the projects from the week to complete

Five Days a Week Schedule				
Day 1	**Day 2**	**Day 3**	**Day 4**	**Day 5**
❑ Read about the Panda ❑ Add information about the panda to the students' Narration Page ❑ Do the Panda Project	❑ Read about the Polar Bear ❑ Add information about the polar bear to the students' Narration Page ❑ Do the Polar Bear Project	❑ Do the Scientific Demonstration: Polar Bears	❑ Read about the Chimpanzee ❑ Add information about the chimpanzee to the students' Narration Page ❑ Do the Chimpanzee Project	❑ Take the Animal Week 6 quiz ❑ Add this week's animals to the Animal Diet Chart (or the Habitat Posters)
All Week Long ❑ Work on memorizing the *Characteristics of Mammals* Poem				

Week 7: Mammals, Part 5 Lesson Plans

Scientific Demonstration: Ear Size

Supplies Needed

- ✓ Paper cups
- ✓ Ticking watch
- ✓ Ruler

Purpose

This demonstration is meant to help the students to see how the size of your ear can affect your hearing.

Instructions and Explanation

The instructions and explanation for this scientific demonstration are found on pp. 58-59 of *Janice VanCleave's Science Around the World*. Have the students complete the Lab Report on SW pg. 21.

Take it Further

Do the additional demonstration described in *Janice VanCleave's Science Around the World* on pg. 59.

Science-Oriented Books

Reading Assignments

- *Kingfisher Encyclopedia of Animals pg. 49 (Kangaroo), pg. 50 (Koala), pg. 52 (Beaver)*
- *DK Encyclopedia of Animals pp. 221-223 (Kangaroo), pg. 226 (Koala), pp. 109-110 (Beaver)*

(Optional) Coordinating animals to study this week: Platypus, Mouse, Otter

Discussion Questions

After reading the selected pages from the encyclopedias, ask the following questions for each of the animals in your discussion time:

- ? What are two things you learned about ________?
- ? What did you find interesting about ________?
- ? What kind of food does a ________ eat?
- ? Where do you usually find a ________?

(Optional) Additional Books

- *Kangaroo (Life Cycle of A...(Heinemann Paperback))* by Angela Royston
- *Kangaroo Island: A Story of an Australian Mallee Forest - a Wild Habitats Book* by Deirdre Langeland
- *Koala (Life Cycle of A...)* by Bobbie Kalman
- *A Koala Is Not a Bear! (Crabapples)* by Hannelore Sotzek

- *Beaver (Life Cycle of A...)* by Bobbie Kalman
- *Beavers* by Helen H. Moore
- *The Adventures of Buddy the Beaver: Buddy Explores the Pond* by Carson Clark and Jim Clark

Notebooking

Writing Assignments

- **Narration Page** – Have the students dictate, copy, or write one to four sentences for each animal on SW pg. 20. You can also have them record what habitat the animal typically lives in and whether the animal is a herbivore, omnivore, or carnivore. (*See Animals Week 3 Lesson Plans for an example.*)

- **(Optional) Lapbook** – Work on Animals #3 Flap-book on pg. 20 from *Biology for the Grammar Stage Lapbooking Templates*. Color the kangaroo, koala, and beaver pictures on the flap-book. Have the students tell you what they have learned about the animals. Then, write for them their favorite piece of information on the inside of the flap-book for each animal.

Vocabulary

The following definition is a guide; the students' definitions do not need to match word for word.

- **Wild Animal** – An animal that is typically found only in the wild. (SW pg. 98)

Multi-week Projects and Activities

Unit Project

- **Animal Diet Chart** – Add the kangaroo, koala, and beaver to the Animal Diet Chart on SW pp. 6-7; pictures for this project are on SW pg. 107. The placement chart for this project can be found in the Appendix on pg. 178.
- **(Optional) Habitat Posters** – This week, add the kangaroo, koala, and beaver to the students' habitat posters. The placement chart for this project can be found in the Appendix on pg. 179.

Projects for this Week

- **Coloring Pages** – You can have the students color the following pages from *Biology for the Grammar Stage Coloring Pages*: Kangaroo pg. 25, Koala pg. 26, Beaver pg. 27.
- **Kangaroo** – Have a kangaroo race! Have your students hop from the start line, down to a point, turn around and hop back to finish the race.
- **Koala** – Have the students make a fused bead koala from the pattern found here:
  - http://www.activityvillage.co.uk/koala_fuse_bead_pattern.htm

  (Note — *If your student knows how to cross-stitch you could have them use the above pattern for a cross-stitch project.*)

✂ **Beaver –** Have the students make a beaver mask by painting a paper plate brown. Once it is dry, cut out two holes for eyes. Then, add two brown felt circles for ears and a black pom-pom for a nose. Finally, cut out two white rectangles and attach them for teeth.

Memorization

Continue to work on memorizing the *Characteristics of Mammals* poem. (SW pg. 100)

Characteristics of Mammals
Mammals love to breathe air
They all have fur or hair
Their blood is warm, almost hot
Their babies drink milk a lot!

Quiz

Weekly Quiz

- "Animal Week 7 Quiz" on SW pg. Q-11.

Quiz Answers

1. True
2. Teeth
3. Strong back legs, long tails
4. Answers will vary

Notes

Possible Schedules for Week 7

Two Days a Week Schedule	
Day 1	**Day 2**
❑ Read about the Koala ❑ Add information about the koala to the students' Narration Page ❑ Do the Scientific Demonstration: Ear Size ❑ Work on memorizing the *Characteristics of Mammals* Poem ❑ Define wild animal	❑ Read about the Kangaroo and Beaver ❑ Complete the students' Narration Page ❑ Add this week's animals to the Animal Diet Chart (or the Habitat Posters) ❑ Take the Animal Week 7 quiz ❑ Choose one of the projects from the week to complete

Five Days a Week Schedule				
Day 1	**Day 2**	**Day 3**	**Day 4**	**Day 5**
❑ Read about the Kangaroo ❑ Add information about the kangaroo to the students' Narration Page ❑ Do the Kangaroo Project	❑ Read about the Koala ❑ Add information about the koala to the students' Narration Page ❑ Do the Koala Project	❑ Do the Scientific Demonstration: Ear Size ❑ Define wild animal	❑ Read about the Beaver ❑ Add information about the beaver to the students' Narration Page ❑ Do the Beaver Project	❑ Take the Animal Week 7 quiz ❑ Add this week's animals to the Animal Diet Chart (or the Habitat Posters)
All Week Long ❑ Work on memorizing the *Characteristics of Mammals* Poem				

Week 8: Mammals, Part 6 Lesson Plans

Scientific Demonstration: Warm-blooded

Supplies Needed

- ✓ Two thermometers
- ✓ 2 Glasses
- ✓ One large bowl

Purpose

This demonstration is meant to help the students to see how animals can lose body heat quicker in water.

Instructions

1. Fill the large bowl with ice cold water.
2. Fill both of the glasses with warm water and record their temperature. This is the initial temperature on your chart.
3. Place one glass in the freezer and one glass in the bowl. (**Be sure that the cold water in the large bowl is covering ¾ of your glass.**)
4. Let both of the glasses sit for 10 minutes.
5. Take the glass out of the freezer and record both temperatures again. Which one was lower?
6. Have the students complete the Lab Report on SW pg. 23.

Explanation

The students should have seen that the glass in the large bowl had a lower temperature. Cold-blooded animals change their temperature with the environment, but warm-blooded animals maintain a constant internal temperature. So, on a hot day, warm-blooded animals need to find a way to quickly get rid of excess heat. One of the ways they do this is by swimming or wading in cold water because heat is transferred quicker through water than it is through air. So, water can be used to lower an animal's temperature quicker than air.

Take it Further

Repeat the demonstration using ice cold water in the glasses instead. This time leave one on the counter and one in a bowl full of room temperature water. (*Once again, you should see that the temperature in the glass is lowered quicker than the one on the counter.*)

Science-Oriented Books

Reading Assignments

- *Kingfisher Encyclopedia of Animals pg. 55 (Armadillo), pg. 58 (Skunk), pg. 65 (Rabbit)*
- *DK Encyclopedia of Animals pg. 99 (Armadillo), pg. 320 (Skunk), pp. 288-289 (Rabbit)*

(Optional) Coordinating animals to study this week: Aardvark, Anteater, Hedgehog, Sloth, Badger, Weasel, Rat, Squirrel

Discussion Questions

After reading the selected pages from the encyclopedias, ask the following questions for each of the animals in your discussion time:

- ? What are two things you learned about _________?
- ? What did you find interesting about _________?
- ? What kind of food does a _________ eat?
- ? Where do you usually find a _________?

(Optional) Additional Books

- *Armadillos (Animals Underground)* by Emily Sebastian
- *Amazing Armadillos (Step into Reading)* by Jennifer Guess McKerley
- *Skunks (Animal Prey)* by Sandra Markle
- *Skunk's Spring Surprise* by Leslea Newman
- *Skunks (Blastoff! Readers: Backyard Wildlife)* by Emily K. Green
- *Rabbits (Blastoff! Readers: Backyard Wildlife)* by Derek Zobel
- *Rabbits and Raindrops* by Jim Arnosky
- *The Little Rabbit* by Judy Dunn
- *The Tale of Peter Rabbit* by Beatrix Potter

Notebooking

Writing Assignments

- **Narration Page** – Have the students dictate, copy, or write one to four sentences for each animal on SW pg. 22. You can also have them record what habitat the animal typically lives in and whether the animal is a herbivore, omnivore, or carnivore. (*See Animals Week 3 Lesson Plans for an example.*)

- **(Optional) Lapbook** – Complete Animals #3 Flap-book on pg. 20 from *Biology for the Grammar Stage Lapbooking Templates*. Color the armadillo, skunk, and rabbit pictures on the flap-book. Have the students tell you what they have learned about the animals. Then, write for them their favorite piece of information on the inside of the flap-book for each animal. Finally, glue the flap-book into the lapbook.

Vocabulary

The following definition is a guide; the students' definitions do not need to match word for word.

- **Vertebrate** – An animal with a backbone. (SW pg. 98)

Multi-week Projects and Activities

Unit Project

- **Animal Diet Chart** – Add the armadillo, skunk, and rabbit to the Animal Diet Chart on SW pp. 6-7; pictures for this project are on SW pg. 107. The placement chart for this project can be found in the Appendix on pg. 178.

- ✂ **(Optional) Habitat Posters** – This week, add the armadillo, skunk, and rabbit to the students' habitat posters. The placement chart for this project can be found in the Appendix on pg. 179.

Projects for this Week

- ✂ **Coloring Pages** – You can have the students color the following pages from *Biology for the Grammar Stage Coloring Pages*: Armadillo pg. 28, Skunk pg. 29, Rabbit pg. 30.
- ✂ **Armadillo** – Make some armadillo potatoes using the recipe from the following website:
  - http://www.food.com/recipe/armadillo-potatoes-180473
- ✂ **Skunk** – Have the students make a clay skunk using the model from the following pin:
  - https://www.pinterest.com/pin/281052832966869442/
- ✂ **Rabbit** – Have the students make a rabbit out of a can by painting the can white. Once it dries, cover it with glue or spray adhesive and glue cotton balls all over the can. Glue pink ears, blue eyes and a pink nose to the end of the can. Then, glue 4 white feet to the side of the can. Finally, draw a face using a permanent marker below the nose and add a few pipe cleaner whiskers.

Memorization

- Continue to work on memorizing the *Characteristics of Mammals* poem. (SW pg. 100)

Characteristics of Mammals
Mammals love to breathe air
They all have fur or hair
Their blood is warm, almost hot
Their babies drink milk a lot!

Quiz

Weekly Quiz

- "Animal Week 8 Quiz" on SW pg. Q-12.

Quiz Answers

1. True
2. A lot of
3. False (*Skunks spray a very smelly scent as a form of defense.*)
4. Answers will vary

Notes

Possible Schedules for Week 8

Two Days a Week Schedule	
Day 1	**Day 2**
❑ Read about the Skunk ❑ Add information about the skunk to the students' Narration Page ❑ Do the Scientific Demonstration: Warm-blooded ❑ Work on memorizing the *Characteristics of Mammals* Poem ❑ Define vertebrate	❑ Read about the Armadillo and Rabbit ❑ Complete the students' Narration Page ❑ Add this week's animals to the Animal Diet Chart (or the Habitat Posters) ❑ Take the Animal Week 8 quiz ❑ Choose one of the projects from the week to complete

Five Days a Week Schedule				
Day 1	**Day 2**	**Day 3**	**Day 4**	**Day 5**
❑ Read about the Armadillo ❑ Add information about the armadillo to the students' Narration Page ❑ Do the Armadillo Project	❑ Read about the Skunk ❑ Add information about the skunk to the students' Narration Page ❑ Do the Skunk Project	❑ Do the Scientific Demonstration: Warm-blooded ❑ Define vertebrate	❑ Read about the Rabbit ❑ Add information about the rabbit to the students' Narration Page ❑ Do the Rabbit Project	❑ Take the Animal Week 8 quiz ❑ Add this week's animals to the Animal Diet Chart (or the Habitat Posters)
All Week Long ❑ Work on memorizing the *Characteristics of Mammals* Poem				

Week 9: Mammals, Part 7 Lesson Plans

Scientific Demonstration: Tangled

Supplies Needed

- ✓ Rubber bands

Purpose

This demonstration is meant to help the students to see the effect of plastic garbage pollution on sea animals.

Instructions and Explanation

The instructions and explanation for this scientific demonstration are found on pp. 136-137 of *Janice VanCleave's Biology for Every Kid*. Have the students complete the Lab Report on SW pg. 25.

Take it Further

Try removing the rubber band with your feet. Do they help?

Science-Oriented Books

Reading Assignments

- *Kingfisher Encyclopedia of Animals pg. 66 (Walrus), pg. 70 (Whale), pg. 71 (Dolphin)*
- *DK Encyclopedia of Animals pg. 350 (Walrus), pp. 353-354 (Whale), pp. 160-162 (Dolphin)*

(Optional) Coordinating animals to study this week: Sea Cow (Manatee), Seal and Sea Lion, Killer Whale

Discussion Questions

After reading the selected pages from the encyclopedias, ask the following questions for each of the animals in your discussion time:

- **?** What are two things you learned about ________?
- **?** What did you find interesting about ________?
- **?** What kind of food does a ________ eat?
- **?** Where do you usually find a ________?

(Optional) Additional Books

- *Little Walrus Warning (Smithsonian Oceanic Collection)* by Carol Young
- *Walruses (Blastoff! Readers: Oceans Alive)* by Colleen A. Sexton
- *Face to Face with Whales (Face to Face with Animals)* by Flip Nicklin
- *Amazing Whales! (I Can Read Book 2)* by Sarah L. Thomson
- *Is a Blue Whale the Biggest Thing There Is? (Robert E. Wells Science)* by Robert E. Wells
- *Face to Face with Dolphins (Face to Face with Animals)* by Flip Nicklin
- *Dolphin Talk: Whistles, Clicks, and Clapping Jaws (Let's-Read-and-Find...)* by Wendy

Pfeffer

Eye Wonder: Whales and Dolphins by Caroline Bingham

Notebooking

Writing Assignments

- **Narration Page** – Have the students dictate, copy, or write one to four sentences for each animal on SW pg. 24. You can also have them record what habitat the animal typically lives in and whether the animal is a herbivore, omnivore, or carnivore. (*See Animals Week 3 Lesson Plans for an example.*)

- **(Optional) Lapbook** – Work on Animals #4 Flap-book on pg. 21 from *Biology for the Grammar Stage Lapbooking Templates*. Color the walrus, whale, and dolphin pictures on the flap-book. Have the students tell you what they have learned about the animals. Then, write for them their favorite piece of information on the inside of the flap-book for each animal.

Vocabulary

The following definition is a guide; the students' definitions do not need to match word for word.

- **Marine Mammal** – An animal that has all the characteristics of a mammal, but that also lives in the water. (SW pg. 95)

Multi-week Projects and Activities

Unit Project

- **Animal Diet Chart** – Add the walrus, whale, and dolphin to the Animal Diet Chart on SW pp. 6-7; pictures for this project are on SW pg. 107. The placement chart for this project can be found in the Appendix on pg. 178.
- **(Optional) Habitat Posters** – This week, add the walrus, whale, and dolphin to the students' habitat posters. The placement chart for this project can be found in the Appendix on pg. 179.

Projects for this Week

- **Coloring Pages** – You can have the students color the following pages from *Biology for the Grammar Stage Coloring Pages*: Walrus pg. 31, Whale pg. 32, Dolphin pg. 33.
- **Walrus** – Have the students make a peek-a-boo walrus using the directions from the following website:
  - http://www.daniellesplace.com/html/Walrus-Crafts-learning-activities.html
- **Whale** – Have the students make a whale water scooper using a rinsed out 2 gallon jug. Begin by mixing 4 parts gray paint and 1 part glue and use the mixture to paint the jug all over. Then, cut out a curved line in the bottom of the jug. Next, glue on two googly eyes just above the curved line on either side of the jug and cut a small blow hole between the eyes and the handle. Finally, cut a long, skinny heart out of a sheet of gray

foam and attach it to the top of the jug for the whale's tail.

✂ **Dolphin –** Have the students try to communicate with each other in dolphin language. In other words, have them figure out a way to express what they want using only clicks and whistles.

Memorization

Continue to work on memorizing the *Characteristics of Mammals* poem. (SW pg. 100)

Characteristics of Mammals
Mammals love to breathe air
They all have fur or hair
Their blood is warm, almost hot
Their babies drink milk a lot!

Quiz

Weekly Quiz

- "Animal Week 9 Quiz" on SW pg. Q-13.

Quiz Answers

1. Biggest
2. True
3. Very
4. Answers will vary

Notes

Possible Schedules for Week 9

Two Days a Week Schedule	
Day 1	**Day 2**
❑ Read about the Dolphin ❑ Add information about the dolphin to the students' Narration Page ❑ Do the Scientific Demonstration: Tangled ❑ Work on memorizing the *Characteristics of Mammals* Poem ❑ Define marine mammal	❑ Read about the Walrus and Whale ❑ Complete the students' Narration Page ❑ Add this week's animals to the Animal Diet Chart (or the Habitat Posters) ❑ Take the Animal Week 9 quiz ❑ Choose one of the projects from the week to complete

Five Days a Week Schedule				
Day 1	**Day 2**	**Day 3**	**Day 4**	**Day 5**
❑ Read about the Walrus ❑ Add information about the walrus to the students' Narration Page ❑ Do the Walrus Project	❑ Read about the Whale ❑ Add information about the whale to the students' Narration Page ❑ Do the Whale Project	❑ Read about the Dolphin ❑ Add information about the dolphin to the students' Narration Page ❑ Do the Dolphin Project	❑ Do the Scientific Demonstration: Tangled ❑ Define marine mammal	❑ Take the Animal Week 9 quiz ❑ Add this week's animals to the Animal Diet Chart (or the Habitat Posters)
All Week Long ❑ Work on memorizing the *Characteristics of Mammals* Poem				

Week 10: Mammals, Part 8 Lesson Plans

Scientific Demonstration: Hairy

Supplies Needed

- ✓ 2 Glass jars
- ✓ Box at least 2 inches wider and taller than the jars
- ✓ Cotton balls
- ✓ 2 Thermometers

Purpose

This demonstration is meant to help the students to see how hair helps to keep an animal warm.

Instructions

1. Fill two glasses with hot water and record the temperature. This is the initial temperature on your chart on SW pg. 27.
2. Leave one glass on the counter and place the other glass in the box. Then, quickly pack the cotton balls around the glass, trying to fill up all the space between the glass and the box.
3. Let both glasses sit for 15 minutes.
4. Then, record the temperatures once again.
5. Have the students complete the Lab Report on SW pg. 27.

Explanation

The students should see that the glass that sat out on the counter should have a lower temperature. This is because the cotton in the box helped to insulate the water in the glass, which prevented it from loosing heat too quickly. The hair on a mammal also acts as an insulator for the animal. It helps them to keep their body temperature from dropping too quickly when they are in a cold environment.

Take it Further

Repeat the demonstration using feathers and wool. (*The students should see that the feathers and wool also act as insulators.*)

Science-Oriented Books

Reading Assignments

- 🕮 *Kingfisher Encyclopedia of Animals pg. 76 (Goat), pg. 77 (Cow and Bull), pg. 81 (Pig)*
- 🕮 *DK Encyclopedia of Animals pg. 191 (Goat), pp. 131-133 (Cow and Bull), pp. 280-281 (Pig)*

(Optional) Coordinating animals to study this week: Antelope, Sheep, Yak, Bison, Buffalo

Discussion Questions

After reading the selected pages from the encyclopedias, ask the following questions for each of the animals in your discussion time:

- ? What are two things you learned about _________?
- ? What did you find interesting about _________?
- ? What kind of food does a _________ eat?
- ? Where do you usually find a _________?

(Optional) Additional Books

- *Goats (Animals That Live on the Farm)* by JoAnn Early Macken
- *Life on a Goat Farm (Life on a Farm)* by Judy Wolfman
- *Little Apple Goat* by Caroline Church
- *Cows and Their Calves (Pebble Plus: Animal Offspring)* by Margaret Hall
- *Raising Cows on the Koebels' Farm (Our Neighborhood)* by Alice K. Flanagan
- *Milk: From Cow to Carton (Let's-Read-and-Find... Book)* by Aliki
- *Pigs (Animals That Live on the Farm)* by JoAnn Early Macken
- *Life on a Pig Farm (Life on a Farm)* by Judy Wolfman
- *The Three Little Pigs*

Notebooking

Writing Assignments

- **Narration Page** – Have the students dictate, copy, or write one to four sentences for each animal on SW pg. 26. You can also have them record what habitat the animal typically lives in and whether the animal is a herbivore, omnivore, or carnivore. (*See Animals Week 3 Lesson Plans for an example.*)

- **(Optional) Lapbook** – Complete Animals #4 Flap-book on pg. 21 from *Biology for the Grammar Stage Lapbooking Templates*. Color the goat, cow, and pig pictures on the flap-book. Have the students tell you what they have learned about the animals. Then, write for them their favorite piece of information on the inside of the flap-book for each animal. Finally, glue the flap-book into the lapbook.

Vocabulary

The following definition is a guide; the students' definitions do not need to match word for word.

- **Domesticated Animal** – An animal that has been under human control for many generations. (SW pg. 92)

Multi-week Projects and Activities

Unit Project

- **Animal Diet Chart** – Add the goat, cow, and pig to the Animal Diet Chart on SW pp. 6-7; pictures for this project are on SW pg. 107. The placement chart for this project can be found in the Appendix on pg. 178.
- **(Optional) Habitat Posters** – This week, add the goat, cow, and pig to the students'

habitat posters. The placement chart for this project can be found in the Appendix on pg. 179.

Projects for this Week

- **Field Trip –** Take the students to visit a working farm this week. While there, have them observe the animals and choose several on which to fill out an Animal Observation Sheet. This sheet can be found in the Appendix of this guide on pg. 187.
- **Coloring Pages –** You can have the students color the following pages from *Biology for the Grammar Stage Coloring Pages*: Goat pg. 34, Cow pg. 35, Pig pg. 36.
- **Goat –** Complete an activity page from the following website:
  - http://www.babygoatfarm.com/Child_Activities.htm
- **Cow –** Make your own butter using the directions from the following video:
  - http://www.youtube.com/watch?v=oropJD0CUxI *(Please preview this website before allowing the students to watch the video to make sure it is appropriate for your group.)*
- **Pig –** Have the students make their own pig out of paper plates and toilet paper rolls using the directions from the following website:
  - http://www.dltk-kids.com/animals/mplatepig.htm

Memorization

- Continue to work on memorizing the *Characteristics of Mammals* poem. (SW pg. 100)

Characteristics of Mammals
Mammals love to breathe air
They all have fur or hair
Their blood is warm, almost hot
Their babies drink milk a lot!

Quiz

Weekly Quiz

- "Animal Week 10 Quiz" on SW pg. Q-14.

Quiz Answers

1. Bulls
2. True
3. Anything
4. Answers will vary

Notes

Possible Schedules for Week 10

Two Days a Week Schedule	
Day 1	**Day 2**
❑ Read about the Goat ❑ Add information about the goat to the students' Narration Page ❑ Do the Scientific Demonstration: Hairy ❑ Work on memorizing the *Characteristics of Mammals* Poem ❑ Define domesticated animal	❑ Read about the Cow and Pig ❑ Complete the students' Narration Page ❑ Add this week's animals to the Animal Diet Chart (or the Habitat Posters) ❑ Take the Animal Week 10 quiz ❑ Choose one of the projects from the week to complete

Five Days a Week Schedule				
Day 1	**Day 2**	**Day 3**	**Day 4**	**Day 5**
❑ Read about the Goat ❑ Add information about the goat to the students' Narration Page ❑ Do the Goat Project	❑ Do the Scientific Demonstration: Hairy ❑ Define domesticated animal	❑ Read about the Cow ❑ Add information about the cow to the students' Narration Page ❑ Do the Cow Project	❑ Read about the Pig ❑ Add information about the pig to the students' Narration Page ❑ Do the Pig Project	❑ Take the Animal Week 10 quiz ❑ Add this week's animals to the Animal Diet Chart (or the Habitat Posters)
All Week Long ❑ Work on memorizing the *Characteristics of Mammals* Poem				

Week 11: Birds, Part 1 Lesson Plans

Scientific Demonstration: Soda Bottle Bird Feeder

Supplies Needed

- ✓ Soda bottle
- ✓ Wood dowel
- ✓ Seeds

Purpose

This demonstration is meant to help the students to see and enjoy the birds that live in your area.

Instructions and Explanation

The instructions and explanation for this scientific demonstration are found on pg. 21 of *Janice VanCleave's Science Around the World*. Have the students complete the Lab Report on SW pg. 29.

Take it Further

During the next four weeks the students can study the birds that visit their bird feeder and keep a journal. If possible, have them take pictures and identify the birds that come to visit it. The students can also turn their journal into a mini-book documenting their bird feeder and birds. I have included a template for a bird feeder mini-book in the Appendix on pp. 188-189 of this guide.

Science-Oriented Books

Reading Assignments

- *Kingfisher Encyclopedia of Animals pg. 84 (Bird), pg. 85 (Eagle), pg. 87 (Owl), pg. 88 (Parrot)*
- *DK Encyclopedia of Animals pp. 115-117 (Bird), pp. 167-168 (Eagle), pp. 267-269 (Owl), pp. 273-274 (Parrot)*

(Optional) Coordinating birds to study this week: Seabird, Vulture, Toucan

Discussion Questions

After reading the selected pages from the encyclopedias, ask the following questions for each of the birds in your discussion time:

- **?** What are two things you learned about ________?
- **?** What did you find interesting about ________?
- **?** What kind of food does a ________ eat?
- **?** Where do you usually find a ________?

(Optional) Additional Books

- *Eagles (Animal Predators)* by Sandra Markle
- *Bald Eagles (Nature Watch (Lerner))* by Charlotte Wilcox

- *Challenger: America's Favorite Eagle* by Margot Theis Raven
- *The Barn Owl (Animal Lives)* by Bert Kitchen
- *White Owl, Barn Owl* by Michael Foreman and Nicola Davies
- *There's an Owl in the Shower* by Jean Craighead George
- *Parrots and Other Birds (Animal Survivors)* by Mary Schulte
- *Parrots (The World's Smartest Animals)* by Ruth Owen
- *Kakapo Rescue: Saving the World's Strangest Parrot (Scientists in the Field Series)* by Sy Montgomery

Notebooking

Writing Assignments

- **Narration Page** – Have the students dictate, copy, or write one to four sentences for each bird on SW pg. 28. You can also have them record what habitat the bird typically lives in and whether the animal is a herbivore, omnivore, or carnivore. (*See Animals Week 3 Lesson Plans for an example.*)

- **(Optional) Lapbook** – Complete Birds #1 Mini-tab Book on pg. 22 from *Biology for the Grammar Stage Lapbooking Templates*. Cut out the pages and color the pictures on the mini-tab book. Have the students tell you what they have learned about the eagle, owl, and parrot. Then, write their favorite piece of information for each of the birds on the pages of the mini-tab book. Finally, glue the booklet into the lapbook.

Vocabulary

The following definition is a guide; the students' definitions do not need to match word for word.

- **Bird** – A warm-blooded, egg-laying, feathered vertebrate; it also has wings. (SW pg. 90)

Multi-week Projects and Activities

Unit Project

- **Animal Diet Chart** – Add the eagle, owl, and parrot to the Animal Diet Chart on SW pp. 6-7; pictures for this project are on SW pg. 107. The placement chart for this project can be found in the Appendix on pg. 178.
- **(Optional) Habitat Posters** – This week, add the eagle, owl, and parrot to the students' habitat posters. The placement chart for this project can be found in the Appendix on pg. 179.

Projects for this Week

- **Coloring Pages** – You can have the students color the following pages from *Biology for the Grammar Stage Coloring Pages*: Eagle pg. 37, Owl pg. 38, Parrot pg. 39.
- **Eagle** – Make a bald eagle using your student's hands and feet. Paint one foot brown, excluding the toes, and use it to make a print in the center of a sheet of paper. Then, paint your student's left hand brown and use it to make a print on the right side of the

foot print (fingers will be pointing down). Repeat with your student's right hand on the left side. Add two googly eyes and some white feathers made of paper for the eagle's head. Finally, cut out a beak from yellow construction paper and glue it on.

- **Owl** – Perform an owl pellet dissection. You can find directions for this project at the following website:
  - http://sassafrasscience.com/owl-pellet-dissection/
- **Parrot** – Have the students make a parrot shaped bird feeder using the directions from the following website:
  - http://www.instructables.com/id/Bird-Feeder-Bird/?ALLSTEPS

Memorization

- This week, begin to work on memorizing the *Characteristics of Birds* poem. (SW pg. 100)

Characteristics of Birds
Birds have wings
Most like to sing
They make beautiful nests
Where they lay eggs and rest

Quiz

Weekly Quiz

- "Animal Week 11 Quiz" on SW pg. Q-15.

Quiz Answers

1. Lays eggs, Has feathers, Warm-blooded
2. False (*Parrots generally live in warm places with lots of sun.*)
3. True
4. True
5. Answers will vary

Notes

Possible Schedules for Week 11

Two Days a Week Schedule	
Day 1	**Day 2**
❑ Read about the Eagle ❑ Add information about the eagle to the students' Narration Page ❑ Do the Scientific Demonstration: Soda Bottle Bird Feeder ❑ Work on memorizing the *Characteristics of Birds* Poem ❑ Define bird	❑ Read about the Owl and Parrot ❑ Complete the students' Narration Page ❑ Add this week's animals to the Animal Diet Chart (or the Habitat Posters) ❑ Take the Animal Week 11 quiz ❑ Choose one of the projects from the week to complete

Five Days a Week Schedule				
Day 1	**Day 2**	**Day 3**	**Day 4**	**Day 5**
❑ Read about the Eagle ❑ Add information about the eagle to the students' Narration Page ❑ Do the Eagle Project	❑ Do the Scientific Demonstration: Soda Bottle Bird Feeder ❑ Define bird	❑ Read about the Owl ❑ Add information about the owl to the students' Narration Page ❑ Do the Owl Project	❑ Read about the Parrot ❑ Add information about the parrot to the students' Narration Page ❑ Do the Parrot Project	❑ Take the Animal Week 11 quiz ❑ Add this week's animals to the Animal Diet Chart (or the Habitat Posters)
All Week Long ❑ Work on memorizing the *Characteristics of Birds* Poem				

Week 12: Birds, Part 2 Lesson Plans

Scientific Demonstration: Oily Feathers

Supplies Needed

- ✓ 1 Quart glass bowl
- ✓ Measuring cup
- ✓ Liquid oil
- ✓ Powdered detergent
- ✓ Measuring spoon

Purpose

This demonstration is meant to help the students to see the effect detergent has on a bird's naturally oily feathers.

Instructions and Explanation

The instructions and explanation for this scientific demonstration are found on pp. 138-139 of *Janice VanCleave's Biology for Every Kid*. Have the students complete the Lab Report on SW pg. 31.

Take it Further

Have the students make a feather collection. They can pick up feathers on a nature walk and identify them before attaching them to a poster. After the feathers are attached, have the students label each sample with the bird that the feather came from and where they found it. If you students are older, you can also have them add a bit of information about the bird.

Science-Oriented Books

Reading Assignments

- *Kingfisher Encyclopedia of Animals pg. 92 (Penguin), pg. 94 (Chicken), pg. 95 (Duck)*
- *DK Encyclopedia of Animals pp. 276-277 (Penguin), pg. 138 (Chicken), pg. 166 (Duck)*

(Optional) Coordinating bird to study this week: Arctic Tern

Discussion Questions

After reading the selected pages from the encyclopedias, ask the following questions for each of the birds in your discussion time:

- **?** What are two things you learned about ________?
- **?** What did you find interesting about ________?
- **?** What kind of food does a ________ eat?
- **?** Where do you usually find a ________?

(Optional) Additional Books

- *Face to Face with Penguins (Face to Face with Animals)* by Yva Momatiuk
- *Emperor Penguin (Life Cycle of A...)* by Bobbie Kalman

- *National Geographic Readers: Penguins!* by Anne Schreiber
- *From Egg to Chicken (How Living Things Grow)* by Anita Ganeri
- *Chickens Aren't the Only Ones (World of Nature Series)* by Ruth Heller
- *Chickens (Animals That Live on the Farm)* by JoAnn Early Macken
- *Ducks and Their Ducklings (Pebble Plus: Animal Offspring)* by Margaret Hall
- *Duck (Life Cycles)* by Louise Spilsbury

Notebooking

Writing Assignments

- **Narration Page** – Have the students dictate, copy, or write one to four sentences for each bird on SW pg. 30. You can also have them record what habitat the bird typically lives in and whether the animal is a herbivore, omnivore, or carnivore. (*See Animals Week 3 Lesson Plans for an example.*)

- **(Optional) Lapbook** – Complete Birds #2 Mini-tab Book on pg. 23 from *Biology for the Grammar Stage Lapbooking Templates*. Cut out the pages and color the pictures on the mini-tab book. Have the students tell you what they have learned about the penguin, chicken, and duck. Then, write their favorite piece of information for each of the birds on the pages of the mini-tab book. Finally, glue the booklet into the lapbook.

Vocabulary

There is no vocabulary for this week.

Multi-week Projects and Activities

Unit Project

- **Animal Diet Chart** – Add the penguin, chicken, and duck to the Animal Diet Chart on SW pp. 6-7; pictures for this project are on SW pg. 107. The placement chart for this project can be found in the Appendix on pg. 178.
- **(Optional) Habitat Posters** – This week, add the penguin, chicken, and duck to the students' habitat posters. The placement chart for this project can be found in the Appendix on pg. 179.

Projects for this Week

- **Coloring Pages** – You can have the students color the following pages from *Biology for the Grammar Stage Coloring Pages*: Penguin pg. 40, Chicken pg. 42, Duck pg. 42.
- **Penguin** – Have the students make a penguin out of egg carton cups using the directions from the following website:
  - http://www.dltk-kids.com/animals/mcarton-penguin.htm
- **Chicken and Duck** – Take a field trip to a local farm where you can see chickens or to a local pond where you can feed the ducks.

Memorization

- Continue to work on memorizing the *Characteristics of Birds* poem. (SW pg. 100)

  <u>Characteristics of Birds</u>
  Birds have wings
  Most like to sing
  They make beautiful nests
  Where they lay eggs and rest

Quiz

Weekly Quiz

- "Animal Week 12 Quiz" on SW pg. Q-16.

Quiz Answers

1. True
2. In the water
3. Weatherproof feathers, Layers of fat
4. Answers will vary

Notes

Possible Schedules for Week 12

Two Days a Week Schedule	
Day 1	**Day 2**
❑ Read about the Penguin ❑ Add information about the penguin to the students' Narration Page ❑ Do the Scientific Demonstration: Oily Feathers ❑ Work on memorizing the *Characteristics of Birds* Poem	❑ Read about the Chicken and Duck ❑ Complete the students' Narration Page ❑ Add this week's animals to the Animal Diet Chart (or the Habitat Posters) ❑ Take the Animal Week 12 quiz ❑ Choose one of the projects from the week to complete

Five Days a Week Schedule				
Day 1	**Day 2**	**Day 3**	**Day 4**	**Day 5**
❑ Read about the Penguin ❑ Add information about the penguin to the students' Narration Page ❑ Do the Eagle Project	❑ Do the Scientific Demonstration: Oily Feathers	❑ Read about the Chicken ❑ Add information about the chicken to the students' Narration Page ❑ Do the Take it Further activity from the Demonstration	❑ Read about the Duck ❑ Add information about the parrot to the students' Narration Page ❑ Do the Chicken/Duck Project	❑ Take the Animal Week 12 quiz ❑ Add this week's animals to the Animal Diet Chart (or the Habitat Posters)
All Week Long ❑ Work on memorizing the *Characteristics of Birds* Poem				

Week 13: Birds, Part 3 Lesson Plans

Scientific Demonstration: Lift Off

Supplies Needed

- ✓ Scissors
- ✓ Notebook paper
- ✓ Ruler

Purpose

This demonstration is meant to help the students to determine why the shape of a bird's wing is important for flight.

Instructions and Explanation

The instructions and explanation for this scientific demonstration are found on pp. 134-135 of *Janice VanCleave's Biology for Every Kid.* Have the students complete the Lab Report on SW pg. 33.

Take it Further

Repeat the demonstration with the students, but this time use different sizes of paper. Is there a difference? You can also try placing the paper in a different spot to see if the results are affected.

Science-Oriented Books

Reading Assignments

- *Kingfisher First Encyclopedia of Animals pg. 96 (Swan), pg. 98 (Swallow), pg. 99 (Hummingbird)*
- *DK Encyclopedia of Animals pp. 334-335 (Swan), pg. 353 (Swallow), pg. 209 (Hummingbird)*

(Optional) Coordinating birds to study this week: Pelican, Sparrow

Discussion Questions

After reading the selected pages from the encyclopedias, ask the following questions for each of the birds in your discussion time:

- ? What are two things you learned about ________?
- ? What did you find interesting about ________?
- ? What kind of food does a ________ eat?
- ? Where do you usually find a ________?

(Optional) Additional Books

- *Swans (Early Bird Nature)* by Lynn M. Stone
- *Six Swans* by Brothers Grimm
- *The Ugly Duckling* by Hans Christian Anderson

- *Swallows In The Birdhouse* by Stephen R. Swinburne
- *The Journey of a Swallow (Lifecycles)* by Carolyn Scrace
- *Swallow (Animal Neighbors)* by Stephen Savage
- *Hummingbirds (Welcome to the World Series)* by Diane Swanson
- *The Bee Hummingbird (Animals of Americas)* by Emma Romeu
- *Hummingbirds: Facts and Folklore from the Americas* by Jeanette Larson

Notebooking

Writing Assignments

- **Narration Page** – Have the students dictate, copy, or write one to four sentences for each bird on SW pg. 32. You can also have them record what habitat the bird typically lives in and whether the animal is a herbivore, omnivore, or carnivore. (*See Animals Week 3 Lesson Plans for an example.*)

- **(Optional) Lapbook** – Complete Birds #3 Mini-tab Book on pg. 24 from *Biology for the Grammar Stage Lapbooking Templates*. Cut out the pages and color the pictures on the mini-tab book. Have the students tell you what they have learned about the swan, swallow, and hummingbird. Then, write their favorite piece of information for each of the birds on the pages of the mini-tab book. Finally, glue the booklet into the lapbook.

Vocabulary

The following definition is a guide; the students' definitions do not need to match word for word.

- **Migration** – A journey made by an animal to a new habitat. (SW pg. 95)

Multi-week Projects and Activities

Unit Project

- **Animal Diet Chart** – Add the swan, swallow, and hummingbird to the Animal Diet Chart on SW pp. 6-7; pictures for this project are on SW pg. 109. The placement chart for this project can be found in the Appendix on pg. 178.
- **(Optional) Habitat Posters** – This week, add the swan, swallow, and hummingbird to the students' habitat posters. The placement chart for this project can be found in the Appendix on pg. 179.

Projects for this Week

- **Coloring Pages** – You can have the students color the following pages from *Biology for the Grammar Stage Coloring Pages*: Swan pg. 43, Swallow pg. 44, Hummingbird pg. 45.
- **Swan** – Have the students make a swan out of a pine cone, pipe cleaner and feathers using the directions from the following website:
  - http://familyfun.go.com/crafts/crafts-by-type/animal-bug-crafts/animal-themed-crafts/bird-crafts/swans-a-swimming-673412/
- **Swallow** – Discuss migration with your students. You can read about it in the main

texts on the following pages:

- *"Migration" Kingfisher First Encyclopedia of Animals pg. 9*
- *"Migration" DK Encyclopedia of Animals pg. 78-79*

Hummingbird - Set up a hummingbird feeder in your backyard and see if you get any visitors.

Memorization

Continue to work on memorizing the *Characteristics of Birds* poem. (SW pg. 100)

Characteristics of Birds
Birds have wings
Most like to sing
They make beautiful nests
Where they lay eggs and rest

Quiz

Weekly Quiz

"Animal Week 13 Quiz" onSW pg. Q-17.

Quiz Answers

1. Very fast
2. True
3. Together
4. Answers will vary

Notes

Possible Schedules for Week 13

Two Days a Week Schedule	
Day 1	**Day 2**
❑ Read about the Swan ❑ Add information about the swan to the students' Narration Page ❑ Do the Scientific Demonstration: Lift Off ❑ Work on memorizing the *Characteristics of Birds* Poem ❑ Define migration	❑ Read about the Swallow and Hummingbird ❑ Complete the students' Narration Page ❑ Add this week's animals to the Animal Diet Chart (or the Habitat Posters) ❑ Take the Animal Week 12 quiz ❑ Choose one of the projects from the week to complete

Five Days a Week Schedule				
Day 1	**Day 2**	**Day 3**	**Day 4**	**Day 5**
❑ Read about the Swan ❑ Add information about the swan to the students' Narration Page ❑ Do the Swan Project	❑ Read about the Swallow ❑ Add information about the swallow to the students' Narration Page ❑ Do the Swallow project	❑ Do the Scientific Demonstration: Lift Off ❑ Define migration	❑ Read about the Hummingbird ❑ Add information about the hummingbird to the students' Narration Page ❑ Do the Hummingbird Project	❑ Take the Animal Week 12 quiz ❑ Add this week's animals to the Animal Diet Chart (or the Habitat Posters)
All Week Long ❑ Work on memorizing the *Characteristics of Birds* Poem				

Week 14: Birds, Part 4 Lesson Plans

Scientific Demonstration: Naked Egg

Supplies Needed

- ✓ 1 Raw egg
- ✓ 1 Jar with a lid
- ✓ White vinegar
- ✓ Measuring tape

Purpose

This demonstration is meant to help the students to see how vinegar affects the eggshell.

Instructions and Explanation

The instructions and explanation for this scientific demonstration are found on pp. 146-147 of *Janice VanCleave's Biology for Every Kid*. Have the students complete the Lab Report on SW pg. 35.

Take it Further

Have the students open up the egg to see if the inside of the egg has changed at all. Compare it to another egg that still has its shell intact and not the similarities and differences. (*The students should see that the insides the two eggs are very similar. They both have a yolk that is surrounded by clear liquid, or albumin. They may see that the egg from the demonstration has more clear liquid than the egg with its shell intact. This is due to osmosis.*)

Science-Oriented Books

Reading Assignments

- *Kingfisher First Encyclopedia of Animals pg. 100 (Flamingo), pg. 101 (Peacock), pg. 103 (Ostrich)*
- *DK Encyclopedia of Animals pg. 275 (Peacock), pp. 261-262 (Ostrich)*

(Optional) Coordinating bird to study this week: Kiwi

Discussion Questions

After reading the selected pages from the encyclopedias, ask the following questions for each of the birds in your discussion time:

- ? What are two things you learned about ________?
- ? What did you find interesting about ________?
- ? What kind of food does a ________ eat?
- ? Where do you usually find a ________?

(Optional) Additional Books

- *Flamingos (Safari Animals)* by Maddie Gibbs
- *A Flamingo Chick Grows Up (Baby Animals (Learner Classroom))* by Joan Hewett
- *The Life Cycle of a Flamingo (Things With Wings)* by JoAnn Early Macken

- *The Peacock's Pride* by Melissa Kajpust
- *Peacocks, Penguins, and Other Birds (Animal Kingdom Classification series)* by Steve Parker
- *How the Peacock Got Its Feathers: Based on a Mayan Tale (Latin American Tales and Myths)* by Sandy Sepehri
- *Ostriches (Safari Animals)* by Maddie Gibbs
- *Ostriches (Animals That Live in the Grasslands)* by Therese Harasymiw
- *Can You Tell an Ostrich from an Emu? (Lightning Bolt Books: Animal Look-Alikes)* by Buffy Silverman

Notebooking

Writing Assignments

- **Narration Page** – Have the students dictate, copy, or write one to four sentences for each bird on SW pg. 34. You can also have them record what habitat the bird typically lives in and whether the animal is a herbivore, omnivore, or carnivore. (*See Animals Week 3 Lesson Plans for an example.*)

- **(Optional) Lapbook** – Complete Birds #4 Mini-tab Book on pg. 25 from *Biology for the Grammar Stage Lapbooking Templates*. Cut out the pages and color the pictures on the mini-tab book. Have the students tell you what they have learned about the flamingo, peacock, and ostrich. Then, write their favorite piece of information for each of the birds on the pages of the mini-tab book. Finally, glue the booklet into the lapbook.

Vocabulary

The following definition is a guide; the students' definitions do not need to match word for word.

- **Egg** – The reproductive structure of some animals. (SW pg. 92)

Multi-week Projects and Activities

Unit Project

- **Animal Diet Chart** – Add the flamingo, peacock, and ostrich to the Animal Diet Chart on SW pp. 6-7; pictures for this project are on SW pg. 109. The placement chart for this project can be found in the Appendix on pg. 178.
- **(Optional) Habitat Posters** – This week, add the flamingo, peacock, and ostrich to the students' habitat posters. The placement chart for this project can be found in the Appendix on pg. 179.

Projects for this Week

- **Coloring Pages** – You can have the students color the following pages from *Biology for the Grammar Stage Coloring Pages*: Flamingo pg. 46, Peacock pg. 47, Ostrich pg. 48.
- **Flamingo** – Have the students make a flamingo out of pipe cleaners, a pom-pom and a small styrofoam ball. Begin by painting the styrofoam ball pink. While it dries, assemble the head by gluing two googly eyes to either side of a pink pom-pom. Then, use a small

piece of a yellow pipe cleaner to make a beak and attach it to the pink pom-pom head. Next, glue a pink pipe cleaner to the pink pom-pom head. Finally, insert the head/neck into the pink styrofoam ball and add two legs made out of two more pink pipe cleaners.

- **Peacock –** Watch the following video from YouTube that shows a peacocks call and full display of its feathers:
  - http://www.youtube.com/watch?v=0C8gLC0OZzk *(Please preview this website before allowing the students to watch the video to make sure it is appropriate for your group.)*
- **Ostrich –** Ostrich eggs are equivalent to about 18-24 chicken eggs. Discuss with your students the difference between the size of an omelet that you normally make and the size of an omelet that could be made from a single ostrich egg. If you're brave enough, try making an ostrich-sized omelet using 18 eggs.

Memorization

- Continue to work on memorizing the *Characteristics of Birds* poem. (SW pg. 100)

Characteristics of Birds
Birds have wings
Most like to sing
They make beautiful nests
Where they lay eggs and rest

Quiz

Weekly Quiz

- "Animal Week 14 Quiz" on SW pg. Q-18.

Quiz Answers

1. True
2. Giant
3. False (*Flamingos get their pink color from the food they eat.*)
4. Answers will vary

Notes

Possible Schedules for Week 14

Two Days a Week Schedule	
Day 1	**Day 2**
❑ Read about the Flamingo ❑ Add information about the flamingo to the students' Narration Page ❑ Do the Scientific Demonstration: Naked Egg ❑ Work on memorizing the *Characteristics of Birds* Poem ❑ Define egg	❑ Read about the Peacock and Ostrich ❑ Complete the students' Narration Page ❑ Add this week's animals to the Animal Diet Chart (or the Habitat Posters) ❑ Take the Animal Week 14 quiz ❑ Choose one of the projects from the week to complete

Five Days a Week Schedule				
Day 1	**Day 2**	**Day 3**	**Day 4**	**Day 5**
❑ Read about the Flamingo ❑ Add information about the flamingo to the students' Narration Page ❑ Do the Flamingo Project	❑ Do the Scientific Demonstration: Naked Egg ❑ Define egg	❑ Read about the Peacock ❑ Add information about the peacock to the students' Narration Page ❑ Do the Peacock Project ❑ Check on the Naked Egg Demonstration	❑ Read about the Ostrich ❑ Add information about the ostrich to the students' Narration Page ❑ Do the Ostrich Project ❑ Check on the Naked Egg Demonstration	❑ Take the Animal Week 14 quiz ❑ Add this week's animals to the Animal Diet Chart (or the Habitat Posters)
All Week Long ❑ Work on memorizing the *Characteristics of Birds* Poem				

Week 15: Reptiles and Amphibians, Part 1 Lesson Plans

Scientific Demonstration: Ground Temperature

Supplies Needed

- ✓ 2 Outdoor thermometers
- ✓ Trowel
- ✓ White towel

Purpose

This demonstration is meant to help the students to determine why desert animals spend their day underground.

Instructions and Explanation

The instructions and explanation for this scientific demonstration are found on pp. 132-133 of *Janice VanCleave's Biology for Every Kid*. Have the students complete the Lab Report on SW pg. 37.

Take it Further

Have the students repeat the demonstration, only this time have them put one thermometer in the shade and one in full sun. (*The students should see that temperature of the thermometer in the shade was cooler than the one in the full sun.*)

Science-Oriented Books

Reading Assignments

- *Kingfisher First Encyclopedia of Animals pg. 106 (Reptile), pg. 107 (Chameleon), pg. 109 (Iguana), pp. 110-111 (Rattlesnake)*
- *DK Encyclopedia of Animals pp. 297-299 (Reptile), pg. 135 (Chameleon), pg. 72 (Iguana), pg. 292 (Rattlesnake)*

(Optional) Coordinating reptiles to study this week: Lizard, Newt, Anaconda, Cobra

Discussion Questions

After reading the selected pages from the encyclopedias, ask the following questions for each of the reptiles in your discussion time:

- **?** What are two things you learned about ________?
- **?** What did you find interesting about ________?
- **?** What kind of food does a ________ eat?
- **?** Where do you usually find a ________?

(Optional) Additional Books

- *Chameleons (Animals of the Rainforest)* by Erika Deiters and Jim Deiters
- *Chameleons and Other Animals with Amazing Skin (Scholastic News Nonfiction Readers)* by Susan LaBella

- *The Mixed-up Chameleon* by Eric Carle
- *101 Facts About Iguanas* by Sarah Williams
- *Iguanas (The World of Reptiles)* by Sophie Lockwood
- *I Wanna Iguana* by Karen Kaufman Orloff
- *What's Inside a Rattlesnake's Rattle? (Kids' Questions)* by Heather Montgomery
- *Rattlesnakes (Animal Predators)* by Sandra Markle
- *Baby Rattlesnake* by Lynn Moroney

Notebooking

Writing Assignments

- **Narration Page** – Have the students dictate, copy, or write one to four sentences for each reptile on SW pg. 36. You can also have them record what habitat the reptile typically lives in and whether the animal is a herbivore, omnivore, or carnivore. (*See Animals Week 3 Lesson Plans for an example.*)

- **(Optional) Lapbook** – Work on the Reptiles Booklet on pp. 26-27 from *Biology for the Grammar Stage Lapbooking Templates.* Cut out the pages and color the pictures on each of the pages in the booklet. Have the students tell you what they have learned about reptiles along with the chameleon, iguana, and rattlesnake. Then, write their favorite piece of information for each page of the booklet.

Vocabulary

The following definition is a guide; the students' definitions do not need to match word for word.

- **Reptile** – A group of cold-blooded animals that usually have rough skin. (SW pg. 96)

Multi-week Projects and Activities

Unit Project

- **Animal Diet Chart** – Add the chameleon, iguana, and rattlesnake to the Animal Diet Chart on SW pp. 6-7; pictures for this project are on SW pg. 109. The placement chart for this project can be found in the Appendix on pg. 178.
- **(Optional) Habitat Posters** – This week, add the chameleon, iguana, and rattlesnake to the students' habitat posters. The placement chart for this project can be found in the Appendix on pg. 179.

Projects for this Week

- **Coloring Pages** – You can have the students color the following pages from *Biology for the Grammar Stage Coloring Pages*: Chameleon pg. 49, Iguana pg. 50, Rattlesnake pg. 51.
- **Chameleon** – Have the students make a colorful chameleon using tissue paper. Begin by printing out the chameleon picture in the Appendix on pg. 190. Have your student glue several different colors of tissue paper on the chameleon. Once it is dry, cut the chameleon out and glue it onto a sheet of green construction paper.

- ✂ **Iguana** – Have the students research and learn more about the Marine Iguana. It lives on the Galapagos Islands and is the only lizard that routinely goes in the ocean. It is able to slow down its heart rate to reduce heat loss as it swims out into the water in search of seaweed to eat.
- ✂ **Rattlesnake** – Have the students make a rattlesnake out of an egg carton, some pipe cleaners and a few beans. Begin by cutting up the egg carton and painting the individual egg cups brown. Once they are dry glue the egg cups along a pipe cleaner so that there is one on top and one on the bottom forming a body segment all along the pipe cleaner. (**Note** — *You may need to use two pipe cleaners.*) In the last segment, add several beans before gluing the two egg cups together. Then, add googly eyes and a red tongue to the beginning of your rattlesnake. Older student may want to also add some rattlesnake designs with paint to their creations.

Memorization

- Work on memorizing the *Characteristics of Reptiles* poem. (SW pg. 100)

<u>Characteristics of Reptiles</u>
Reptiles like meat
Their blood is cold - sweet!
They have scaly, watertight skin
And in their nests their eggs lay in.

Quiz

Weekly Quiz

- "Animal Week 15 Quiz" on SW pg. Q-19.

Quiz Answers

1. Cold-blooded, Lays eggs, Has rough skin
2. False (*Chameleons can change their color to blend into their environment.*)
3. True
4. False (*Rattlesnakes can shake their tail and produce noise.*)
5. Answers will vary

Notes

Possible Schedules for Week 15

Two Days a Week Schedule	
Day 1	**Day 2**
❑ Read about Reptiles and Iguanas ❑ Add information about the iguana to the students' Narration Page ❑ Do the Scientific Demonstration: Ground Temperature ❑ Work on memorizing the *Characteristics of Reptiles* Poem ❑ Define reptile	❑ Read about the Chameleon and Rattlesnake ❑ Complete the students' Narration Page ❑ Add this week's animals to the Animal Diet Chart (or the Habitat Posters) ❑ Take the Animal Week 15 quiz ❑ Choose one of the projects from the week to complete

Five Days a Week Schedule				
Day 1	**Day 2**	**Day 3**	**Day 4**	**Day 5**
❑ Read about the Iguana ❑ Add information about the iguana to the students' Narration Page ❑ Do the Iguana Project	❑ Do the Scientific Demonstration: Ground Temperature ❑ Define reptile	❑ Read about the Chameleon ❑ Add information about the chameleon to the students' Narration Page ❑ Do the Chameleon Project	❑ Read about the Rattlesnake ❑ Add information about the rattlesnake to the students' Narration Page ❑ Do the Rattlesnake Project	❑ Take the Animal Week 15 quiz ❑ Add this week's animals to the Animal Diet Chart (or the Habitat Posters)
All Week Long ❑ Work on memorizing the *Characteristics of Reptiles* Poem				

Week 16: Reptiles and Amphibians, Part 2 Lesson Plans

Scientific Demonstration: Life Cycle of a Frog

Supplies Needed

- ✓ Life Cycle of a Frog (SW pg. 39)

Purpose

This demonstration is meant to help the students to see the changes that a frog goes through during its life time.

Instructions and Explanation

Have the students fill in the life cycle of a frog as you explain it to them. Use the sheet below as a guide.

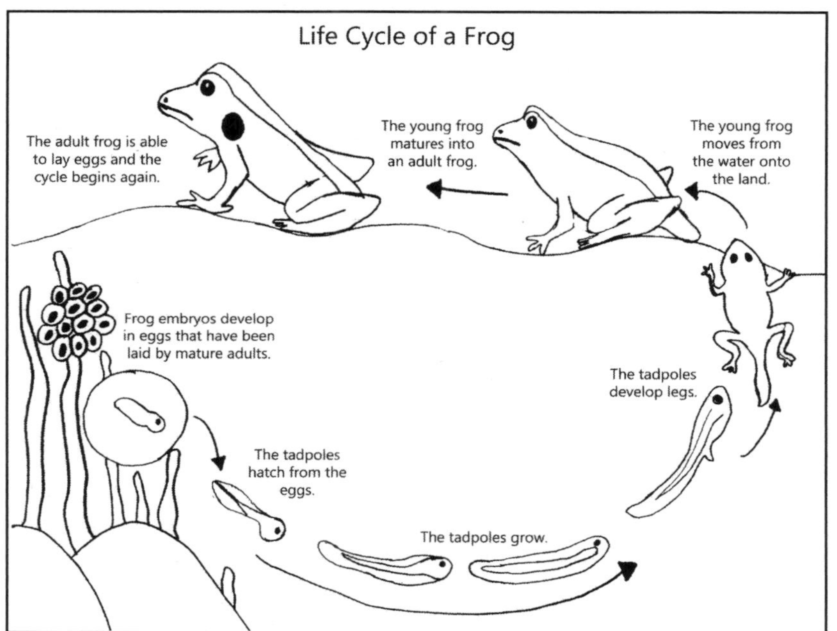

If your students are younger, simply have them write:

1. Eggs;
2. Tadpole;
3. Grows legs;
4. Moves onto land;
5. Adult frog.

After the sheet is filled, have the students color it.

Take it Further

Give the students a chance to see the life cycle of a frog in action by raising a tadpole. You can purchase a kit from Home Science Tools or Amazon.

Science-Oriented Books

Reading Assignments

- *Kingfisher First Encyclopedia of Animals pg. 112 (Alligator and Crocodile), pg. 113 (Turtle), pg. 114 (Amphibian), pg. 115 (Frog)*
- *DK Encyclopedia of Animals pp. 150-152 (Alligator and Crocodile), pp. 342-343 (Turtle), pp. 92-94 (Amphibian), pp. 181-182 (Frog)*

(Optional) Coordinating amphibian to study this week: Salamander

Discussion Questions

After reading the selected pages from the encyclopedias, ask the following questions for each of the reptiles and amphibians in your discussion time:

- **?** What are two things you learned about ________?
- **?** What did you find interesting about ________?
- **?** What kind of food does a ________ eat?
- **?** Where do you usually find a ________?

(Optional) Additional Books

- *Who Lives in an Alligator Hole? (Let's-Read-and-Find... Science 2)* by Anne Rockwell
- *What's the Difference Between an Alligator and a Crocodile? (What's the Difference? (Capstone))* by Lisa Bullard
- *Alligators (Blastoff! Readers: Animal Safari)* by Derek Zobel
- *Look Out for Turtles! (Let's-Read-and-Find... Science 2)* by Melvin Berger
- *Endangered Sea Turtles (Earth's Endangered Animals)* by Bobbie Kalman
- *Turtle Splash!: Countdown at the Pond* by Cathryn Falwell
- *From Tadpole to Frog (Let's-Read-and-Find... Science 1)* by Wendy Pfeffer
- *Frogs and Toads and Tadpoles, Too (Rookie Read-About Science)* by Allan Fowler
- *National Geographic Readers: Frogs!* by Elizabeth Carney

Notebooking

Writing Assignments

- ☐ **Narration Page –** Have the students dictate, copy, or write one to four sentences for each reptile and amphibian on SW pg. 38. You can also have them record what habitat the reptile typically lives in and whether the animal is a herbivore, omnivore, or carnivore. (*See Animals Week 3 Lesson Plans for an example.*)

- ☐ **(Optional) Lapbook –** Finish the Reptiles and Amphibians Booklets on pp. 28-29 from *Biology for the Grammar Stage Lapbooking Templates*. Cut out the pages and color the pictures on each of the pages in the booklet. Have the students tell you what they have learned about amphibians along with the alligators, turtles, and frogs. Then, write their favorite piece of information for each page of the booklet.

Vocabulary

The following definition is a guide; the students' definitions do not need to match word for word.

- **Amphibian –** A cold-blooded, smooth-skinned vertebrate, such as a frog or salamander. (SW pg. 90)

Multi-week Projects and Activities

Unit Project

- **Animal Diet Chart –** Add the alligators, turtles, and frogs to the Animal Diet Chart on SW pp. 6-7; pictures for this project are on SW pg. 109. The placement chart for this project can be found in the Appendix on pg. 178.
- **(Optional) Habitat Posters –** This week, add the alligators, turtles, and frogs to the students' habitat posters. The placement chart for this project can be found in the Appendix on pg. 179.

Projects for this Week

- **Coloring Pages –** You can have the students color the following pages from *Biology for the Grammar Stage Coloring Pages*: Alligator pg. 52, Turtle pg. 53, Frog pg. 54.
- **Alligator –** Have the students make a paper mache alligator using the directions from the following website:
  - http://www.dltk-kids.com/animals/malligator.html
- **Turtle –** Have the students make their own baby turtles using the directions from the following website:
  - http://www.busybeekidscrafts.com/Baby-Pet-Turtles.html

Memorization

- Continue to work on memorizing the *Characteristics of Amphibians* poem. (SW pg. 100)

<u>Characteristics of Amphibians</u>
Amphibians can live on water or land
They lay eggs and have cold blood - grand!

Quiz

Weekly Quiz

- "Animal Week 16 Quiz" on SW pg. Q-20.

Quiz Answers

1. True
2. False (*Frogs and toads are both amphibians.*)
3. A heavy shell
4. True
5. Answers will vary

Possible Schedules for Week 16

Two Days a Week Schedule	
Day 1	**Day 2**
❑ Read about Amphibians and Frogs ❑ Add information about the frog to the students' Narration Page ❑ Do the Scientific Demonstration: Life Cycle of aFrog ❑ Work on memorizing the *Characteristics of Amphibians* Poem ❑ Define amphibians	❑ Read about the Alligator and Turtle ❑ Complete the students' Narration Page ❑ Add this week's animals to the Animal Diet Chart (or the Habitat Posters) ❑ Take the Animal Week 16 quiz ❑ Choose one of the projects from the week to complete

Five Days a Week Schedule				
Day 1	**Day 2**	**Day 3**	**Day 4**	**Day 5**
❑ Read about the Alligator ❑ Add information about the alligator to the students' Narration Page ❑ Do the Alligator Project	❑ Read about the Turtle ❑ Add information about the turtle to the students' Narration Page ❑ Do the Turtle Project	❑ Read about Amphibians and Frogs ❑ Add information about the frog to the students' Narration Page ❑ Do the Take it Further activity	❑ Do the Scientific Demonstration: Life Cycle of a Frog ❑ Define amphibian	❑ Take the Animal Week 16 quiz ❑ Add this week's animals to the Animal Diet Chart (or the Habitat Posters)
All Week Long ❑ Work on memorizing the *Characteristics of Amphibians* Poem				

Notes

Week 17: Fish Lesson Plans

Scientific Demonstration: Equal Pressure

Supplies Needed

- ✓ Salt
- ✓ Measuring spoon
- ✓ 2 Shallow bowls
- ✓ 1 Small cucumber
- ✓ Masking tape
- ✓ Marker

Purpose

This demonstration is meant to help the students to see how fish cells respond to fresh and salty water.

Instructions and Explanation

The instructions and explanation for this scientific demonstration are found on pp. 114-115 of *Janice VanCleave's Biology for Every Kid*. Have the students complete the Lab Report on SW pg. 41.

Take it Further

Visit an aquarium with your students or set up your own in your house.

Science-Oriented Books

Reading Assignments

- *Kingfisher First Encyclopedia of Animals pg. 118 (Fish), pg. 120 (Salmon/Trout), pg. 122 (Seahorse), pg. 123 (Shark)*
- *DK Encyclopedia of Animals pp. 174-176 (Fish), pp. 310-311 (Seahorse), pp. 315-317 (Shark)*

(Optional) Coordinating fish to study this week: Swordfish, Ray

Discussion Questions

After reading the selected pages from the encyclopedias, ask the following questions for each of the fish in your discussion time:

- **?** What are two things you learned about ________?
- **?** What did you find interesting about ________?
- **?** What kind of food does a ________ eat?
- **?** Where do you usually find a ________?

(Optional) Additional Books

- *What's It Like to Be a Fish? (Let's-Read-and-Find... Science 1)* by Wendy Pfeffer
- *Where Fish Go In Winter* by Amy Goldman Koss and Laura J. Bryant
- *The Life Cycle of Fish (Life Cycles)* by Darlene R. Stille

- *Sea Horse (Life Cycle of A...)* by Bobbie Kalman
- *Project Seahorse (Scientists in the Field Series)* by Pamela S. Turner
- *Mister Seahorse* by Eric Carle
- *Face to Face With Sharks (Face to Face with Animals)* by David Doubilet
- *Shark (Life Cycle of A...)* by John Crossingham
- *National Geographic Readers: Sharks! (Science Reader Level 2)* by Anne Schreiber

Notebooking

Writing Assignments

- **Narration Page** – Have the students dictate, copy, or write one to four sentences for each fish on SW pg. 40. You can also have them record what habitat the fish typically lives in and whether the animal is a herbivore, omnivore, or carnivore. (*See Animals Week 3 Lesson Plans for an example.*)

- **(Optional) Lapbook** – Complete the Fish Wheel on pg. 30 from *Biology for the Grammar Stage Lapbooking Templates*. Cut out the pages and color the pictures. Have the students tell you what they have learned about the salmon, seahorse, and shark. Then, write their favorite piece of information next to each of the animals on the wheel. Let the students decorate the cover before assembling the wheel. Once they are done, assemble the wheel-book with a brad fastener and glue it into the lapbook.

Vocabulary

The following definition is a guide; the students' definitions do not need to match word for word.

- **Fish** – A cold-blooded, aquatic vertebrate with gills and fins; it typically also has an elongated body covered with scales. (SW pg. 93)

Multi-week Projects and Activities

Unit Project

- **Animal Diet Chart** – Add the salmon, seahorse, and shark to the Animal Diet Chart on SW pp. 6-7; pictures for this project are on SW pg. 109. The placement chart for this project can be found in the Appendix on pg. 178.
- **(Optional) Habitat Posters** – This week, add the salmon, seahorse, and shark to the students' habitat posters. The placement chart for this project can be found in the Appendix on pg. 179.

Projects for this Week

- **Coloring Pages** – You can have the students color the following pages from *Biology for the Grammar Stage Coloring Pages*: Salmon pg. 55, Seahorse pg. 56, Shark pg. 57.
- **Salmon** – Go fishing! Begin by cutting out 5 red, 4 blue, 3 green and 2 yellow fish. Attach a paper clip to the end of each of the fish and place them all into a bucket or box that is not see through. Next, tie a magnet to a string and tie the string to a pole, either

a dowel rod or a cardboard tube. Then go fishing and see what you catch. The red fish are worth 1 point each, the blue fish are worth 2 points each, the green fish are worth 5 points each and the yellow fish are worth 10 points each. The person with the most points wins the game.

- ✂ **Seahorse –** Seahorses are very interesting creatures, especially in how they incubate their eggs. Instead of laying their eggs and having the female sit on them, the male carries the eggs in a special brooding pouch. Spend some time during this lesson discussing animal reproduction with your students. You can read about it in the main texts on the following pages:
  - *Kingfisher First Encyclopedia of Animals pg. 15 (Reproduction)*
  - *DK Encyclopedia of Animals pp. 38-43 (Courtship and Mating, First Life, Eggs and Nests)*
- ✂ **Shark –** Have the students make a shark totem pole or mask using the templates found at the following website:
  - http://www.montereybayaquarium.org/lc/teachers_place/resources_learning.aspx

Memorization

- Work on memorizing the *Characteristics of Fish* poem. (SW pg. 101)

<u>Characteristics of Fish</u>
Fish swim in the sea with the otter
Using their gills to breathe in the water
They lay eggs that float through the ocean
And their strong skeletons keep them in motion

Quiz

Weekly Quiz

- "Animal Week 17 Quiz" on SW pg. Q-21.

Quiz Answers

1. Cold-blooded, Has gills, Covered with scales
2. False (*Salmon swim upstream during spawning.*)
3. True
4. True
5. Answers will vary

Notes

Possible Schedules for Week 17

Two Days a Week Schedule	
Day 1	**Day 2**
❑ Read about Fish and Salmon ❑ Add information about the salmon to the students' Narration Page ❑ Do the Scientific Demonstration: Equal Pressure ❑ Work on memorizing the *Characteristics of Fish* Poem ❑ Define fish	❑ Read about the Seahorse and Shark ❑ Complete the students' Narration Page ❑ Add this week's animals to the Animal Diet Chart (or the Habitat Posters) ❑ Take the Animal Week 17 quiz ❑ Choose one of the projects from the week to complete

Five Days a Week Schedule				
Day 1	**Day 2**	**Day 3**	**Day 4**	**Day 5**
❑ Read about Fish and Salmon ❑ Add information about the salmon to the students' Narration Page ❑ Do the Salmon Project	❑ Do the Scientific Demonstration: Equal Pressure ❑ Define fish	❑ Read about the Seahorse ❑ Add information about the seahorse to the students' Narration Page ❑ Do the Seahorse Project	❑ Read about the Shark ❑ Add information about the shark to the students' Narration Page ❑ Do the Shark Project	❑ Take the Animal Week 17 quiz ❑ Add this week's animals to the Animal Diet Chart (or the Habitat Posters)
All Week Long ❑ Work on memorizing the *Characteristics of Fish* Poem				

Week 18: Invertebrates, part 1 Lesson Plans

Scientific Demonstration: Holding On

Supplies Needed

- ✓ Suction cup
- ✓ Rock

Purpose

This demonstration is meant to help the students to see how some sea organisms attach themselves to rocks.

Instructions and Explanation

The instructions and explanation for this scientific demonstration are found on pp. 116-117 of *Janice VanCleave's Biology for Every Kid*. Have the students complete the Lab Report on SW pg. 43.

Take it Further

Repeat the demonstration with several different sized rocks. Have the students see how many suction cups it takes to pick up the various sizes. (*The students should see that the bigger the rock, the more suction they need to pick it up.*)

Science-Oriented Books

Reading Assignments

- 🕮 *Kingfisher First Encyclopedia of Animals pg. 126 (Worm), pg. 127 (Slug and Snail), pg. 129 (Octopus)*
- 🕮 *DK Encyclopedia of Animals pp. 215-216 (Invertebrate), pg. 360 (Worm), pg. 323 (Slug and Snail), pp. 255-257 (Octopus)*

(Optional) Coordinating invertebrates to study this week: Centipede, Starfish

Discussion Questions

After reading the selected pages from the encyclopedias, ask the following questions for each of the invertebrates in your discussion time:

- **?** What are two things you learned about ________?
- **?** What did you find interesting about ________?
- **?** What kind of food does a ________ eat?
- **?** Where do you usually find a ________?

(Optional) Additional Books

- 🕮 *Wiggling Worms at Work (Let's-Read-and-Find... Science 2)* by Wendy Pfeffer
- 🕮 *Diary of a Worm* by Doreen Cronin
- 🕮 *Worms (First Step Nonfiction)* by Robin Nelson
- 🕮 *Are You a Snail? (Backyard Books)* by Judy Allen
- 🕮 *Life of the Snail (Nature Watch)* by Theres Buholzer

- *Tiny Snail* by Tammy Carter Bronson
- *An Octopus Is Amazing (Let's-Read-and-Find... Science, Stage 2)* by Patricia Lauber
- *Octopus (Day in the Life: Sea Animals)* by Louise Spilsbury
- *Good Thing You're Not an Octopus!* by Julie Markes and Maggie Smith

Notebooking

Writing Assignments

- **Narration Page** – Have the students dictate, copy, or write one to four sentences for each invertebrate on SW pg. 42. You can also have them record what habitat the invertebrate typically lives in and whether the animal is a herbivore, omnivore, or carnivore. (*See Animals Week 3 Lesson Plans for an example.*)

- **(Optional) Lapbook** – Work on the Invertebrate Accordion Fold-book on pg. 31 from *Biology for the Grammar Stage Lapbooking Templates*. Cut out the page and color the pictures of the worm, snail, and octopus. Have the students tell you what they have learned about the worm, snail, and octopus. Then, write their favorite piece of information next to each of the animals on the page.

Vocabulary

The following definition is a guide; the students' definitions do not need to match word for word.

- **Invertebrate** – An animal without a backbone. (SW pg. 94)

Multi-week Projects and Activities

Unit Project

- **Animal Diet Chart** – Add the worm, snail, and octopus to the Animal Diet Chart on SW pp. 6-7; pictures for this project are on SW pg. 109. The placement chart for this project can be found in the Appendix on pg. 178.
- **(Optional) Habitat Posters** – This week, add the worm, snail, and octopus to the students' habitat posters. The placement chart for this project can be found in the Appendix on pg. 179.

Projects for this Week

- **Coloring Pages** – You can have the students color the following pages from *Biology for the Grammar Stage Coloring Pages*: Worm pg. 58, Snail pg. 59, Octopus pg. 60.
- **Worm** – Observe a worm farm. You can purchase a pre-made one complete with the worms or make your own using the directions from the following website:
  - http://working-worms.com/content/view/40/62/
- **Snail** – Have the students make a snail habitat. Begin by soaking a small unglazed clay pot in water overnight. The next day in the afternoon, set your pot upside down in your garden and prop up one side with a small rock. Try to set your pot in a shaded place that has a fair amount of foliage nearby. The next morning check your pot to see if any snails

have made their home there.

- **Octopus –** Make octopus hot dogs. Begin by cutting a hot dog two-thirds of the way up several times to create legs. Then, cook the hot dog on the stove according to the package instructions. Serve with your student's favorite side!

Memorization

- Work on memorizing the *Characteristics of Invertebrates* poem. (SW pg. 101)

<u>Characteristics of Invertebrates</u>
Invertebrates have no backbone
They live worldwide, in every zone
Ninety-seven percent of animals are in this group
Like the clams and shrimp that end up in your soup

Quiz

Weekly Quiz

- "Animal Week 18 Quiz" onSW pg. Q-22.

Quiz Answers

1. Without
2. True
3. Both in land and in water
4. 8
5. Answers will vary

Notes

Possible Schedules for Week 18

Two Days a Week Schedule	
Day 1	**Day 2**
❑ Read about Invertebrates and Octopus ❑ Add information about the octopus to the students' Narration Page ❑ Do the Scientific Demonstration: Holding On ❑ Work on memorizing the *Characteristics of Invertebrates* Poem ❑ Define invertebrate	❑ Read about the Worm and Snail ❑ Complete the students' Narration Page ❑ Add this week's animals to the Animal Diet Chart (or the Habitat Posters) ❑ Take the Animal Week 18 quiz ❑ Choose one of the projects from the week to complete

Five Days a Week Schedule				
Day 1	**Day 2**	**Day 3**	**Day 4**	**Day 5**
❑ Read about Invertebrates and Worms ❑ Add information about the worm to the students' Narration Page ❑ Do the Worm Project	❑ Read about the Snail ❑ Add information about the snail to the students' Narration Page ❑ Do the Snail Project	❑ Read about the Octopus ❑ Add information about the octopus to the students' Narration Page ❑ Do the Octopus Project	❑ Do the Scientific Demonstration: Holding On ❑ Define invertebrate	❑ Take the Animal Week 18 quiz ❑ Add this week's animals to the Animal Diet Chart (or the Habitat Posters)
All Week Long ❑ Work on memorizing the *Characteristics of Invertebrates* Poem				

Week 19: Invertebrates, part 2 Lesson Plans

Scientific Demonstration: Telegraph Lines

Supplies Needed

- ✓ String
- ✓ A partner

Purpose

This demonstration is meant to help the students to see how a spider evaluates the size of an intruder.

Instructions and Explanation

The instructions and explanation for this scientific demonstration are found on pp. 102-103 of *Janice VanCleave's Biology for Every Kid*. Have the students complete the Lab Report on SW pg. 45.

Take it Further

Complete the activity "Geometric Designs" on pp. 100-101 of *Janice VanCleave's Biology for Every Kid*.

Science-Oriented Books

Reading Assignments

- *Kingfisher First Encyclopedia of Animals pg. 131 (Shellfish and Shrimp), pg. 132 (Crab), pg. 133 (Spider)*
- *DK Encyclopedia of Animals pp. 147-149 (Crab), pp. 327-328 (Spider)*

(Optional) Coordinating invertebrates to study this week: Lobster, Scorpion, Fly

Discussion Questions

After reading the selected pages from the encyclopedias, ask the following questions for each of the invertebrates in your discussion time:

- **?** What are two things you learned about ________?
- **?** What did you find interesting about ________?
- **?** What kind of food does a ________ eat?
- **?** Where do you usually find a ________?

(Optional) Additional Books

- *Shrimp (Blastoff! Readers: Oceans Alive)* by Colleen A. Sexton
- *Shrimp (Underwater World)* by Deborah Coldiron
- *A Day on a Shrimp Boat* by Ching Yeung Russell
- *Crab (Welcome Books: Ocean Life)* by Lloyd G. Douglas
- *In One Tidepool: Crabs, Snails, and Salty Tails* by Anthony D. Fredericks
- *Clumsy Crab* by Ruth Galloway
- *Time For Kids: Spiders!*

- *Spinning Spiders (Let's-Read-and-Find... Science 2)* by Melvin Berger
- *The Very Busy Spider* by Eric Carle
- *Diary of a Spider* by Doreen Cronin

Notebooking

Writing Assignments

- ☐ **Narration Page** – Have the students dictate, copy, or write one to four sentences for each invertebrate on SW pg. 44. You can also have them record what habitat the invertebrate typically lives in and whether the animal is a herbivore, omnivore, or carnivore. (*See Animals Week 3 Lesson Plans for an example.*)
- ☐ **(Optional) Lapbook** – Complete the Invertebrate Accordion Fold-book on pg. 31 from *Biology for the Grammar Stage Lapbooking Templates*. Color the remaining pictures. Have the students tell you what they have learned about the shrimp and crab. Then, write their favorite piece of information next to each animal on the page. Fold the page and glue it into the lapbook.
- ☐ **(Optional) Lapbook** – Complete the Spider Mini-book on pg. 32 from *Biology for the Grammar Stage Lapbooking Templates*. Cut out the mini-book and color the picture. Have the students tell you what they have learned about the spider. Then, write their favorite piece of information inside the mini-book and glue it into the lapbook.

Vocabulary

The following definition is a guide; the students' definitions do not need to match word for word.

- **Shellfish** – An aquatic invertebrate animal having a shell. (SW pg. 97)

Multi-week Projects and Activities

Unit Project

- ✂ **Animal Diet Chart** – Add the shrimp, crab, and spider to the Animal Diet Chart on SW pp. 6-7; pictures for this project are on SW pg. 109. The placement chart for this project can be found in the Appendix on pg. 178.
- ✂ **(Optional) Habitat Posters** – This week, add the shrimp, crab, and spider to the students' habitat posters. The placement chart for this project can be found in the Appendix on pg. 179.

Projects for this Week

- ✂ **Coloring Pages** – You can have the students color the following pages from *Biology for the Grammar Stage Coloring Pages*: Shrimp pg. 61, Crab pg. 62, Spider pg. 63.
- ✂ **Shrimp** – Examine brine shrimp. Begin by purchasing some brine shrimp from your local pet store. Place them in a shallow dish with a bit of water and use a magnifying glass to observe them. If you have a microscope, make a quick wet mount side so that your students can observe the brine shrimp under the microscope. You can make your

own wet mount slide by following these directions:

1. Place your sample on the slide. (**Note** — *Make sure your sample is very thin or else your cover slip will wobble and you won't get a very good view of your sample.*)
2. Place one drop of water over your sample. (**Note** — *Make sure not to use too much water or else your cover slip will float away and you won't be able to see your sample, either.*)
3. Place the cover slip at a 45 degree angle with one edge touching the water and let go. Your slide is ready to be viewed.

✂ **Crab –** Sew your own crab stuffed animal using the directions found at the following website:

- http://www.craftideas.info/html/bean_bag_crab_c.html

✂ **Spider –** Have the students make a spider out of black pipe clears and Styrofoam balls. Begin by painting one small and one large Styrofoam ball black. Once they are dry, add googly eyes to the smaller Styrofoam ball for the head and attach it to the larger ball using a small piece of pipe cleaner. Then, cut 4 pipe cleaners in half and attach them to either side of the large Styrofoam ball for the eight spider legs.

Memorization

- Continue to work on memorizing the *Characteristics of Invertebrates* poem. (SW pg. 101)

<u>Characteristics of Invertebrates</u>
Invertebrates have no backbone
They live worldwide, in every zone
Ninety-seven percent of animals are in this group
Like the clams and shrimp that end up in your soup

Quiz

Weekly Quiz

- "Animal Week 19 Quiz" on SW pg. Q-23.

Quiz Answers

1. False (*Shellfish are aquatic animals with shells.*)
2. Pinchers
3. True
4. 6
5. Answers will vary

Notes

Possible Schedules for Week 19

Two Days a Week Schedule	
Day 1	**Day 2**
❑ Read about the Spider ❑ Add information about the spider to the students' Narration Page ❑ Do the Scientific Demonstration: Telegraph Lines ❑ Work on memorizing the *Characteristics of Invertebrates* Poem	❑ Read about the Shrimp and Crab ❑ Complete the students' Narration Page ❑ Define shellfish ❑ Add this week's animals to the Animal Diet Chart (or the Habitat Posters) ❑ Take the Animal Week 19 quiz ❑ Choose one of the projects from the week to complete

Five Days a Week Schedule				
Day 1	**Day 2**	**Day 3**	**Day 4**	**Day 5**
❑ Read about the Shrimp ❑ Add information about the shrimp to the students' Narration Page ❑ Do the Shrimp Project	❑ Read about the Crab ❑ Add information about the crab to the students' Narration Page ❑ Do the Crab Project	❑ Read about the Spider ❑ Add information about the spider to the students' Narration Page ❑ Do the Spider Project	❑ Do the Scientific Demonstration: Telegraph Lines ❑ Define shellfish	❑ Take the Animal Week 19 quiz ❑ Add this week's animals to the Animal Diet Chart (or the Habitat Posters)
All Week Long ❑ Work on memorizing the *Characteristics of Invertebrates* Poem				

Week 20: Invertebrates, part 3 Lesson Plans

Scientific Demonstration: Butterfly Glider

Supplies Needed

- ✓ Paper clip
- ✓ Printout from pg. 32 of *Science Around The World*
- ✓ Paint for the butterfly
- ✓ Construction paper

Purpose

This demonstration is meant to help the students to see how some sea organisms attach themselves to rocks.

Instructions and Explanation

The instructions and explanation for this scientific demonstration are found on pg. 32 of *Janice VanCleave's Science Around the World*. Have the students complete the Lab Report on SW pg. 47.

Take it Further

Complete the activity "Distinctive" on pp. 98-99 of *Janice VanCleave's Biology for Every Kid*.

Science-Oriented Books

Reading Assignments

- 🕮 *Kingfisher First Encyclopedia of Animals pg. 134 (Insect), pg. 135 (Ant), pg. 138 (Butterfly), pg. 140 (Grasshopper)*
- 🕮 *DK Encyclopedia of Animals pp. 212-214 (Insect), pg. 96 (Ant), pp. 121-123 (Butterfly), pp. 195-196 (Grasshopper)*

(Optional) Coordinating invertebrates to study this week: Bee, Beetle, Dragonfly

Discussion Questions

After reading the selected pages from the encyclopedias, ask the following questions for each of the insects in your discussion time:

- ? What are two things you learned about ________?
- ? What did you find interesting about ________?
- ? What kind of food does a ________ eat?
- ? Where do you usually find a ________?

(Optional) Additional Books

- 🕮 *Ant Cities (Let's-Read-and-Find... Science 2)* by Arthur Dorros
- 🕮 *National Geographic Readers: Ants* by Melissa Stewart
- 🕮 *Are You an Ant? (Backyard Books)* by Judy Allen
- 🕮 *From Caterpillar to Butterfly (Let's-Read-and-Find...)* by Deborah Heiligman

- *National Geographic Readers: Great Migrations Butterflies* by Laura F. Marsh
- *Caterpillars and Butterflies (Usborne Beginners)* by Stephanie Turnbull
- *Life of a Grasshopper (Life Cycles (Raintree Paperback))* by Clare Hibbert
- *Grasshoppers (Bugs Bugs Bugs)* by Margaret Hall
- *Are You a Grasshopper? (Backyard Books)* by Judy Allen

Notebooking

Writing Assignments

- **Narration Page** – Have the students dictate, copy, or write one to four sentences for each insect on SW pg. 46. You can also have them record what habitat the invertebrate typically lives in and whether the animal is a herbivore, omnivore, or carnivore. (*See Animals Week 3 Lesson Plans for an example.*)

- **(Optional) Lapbook** – Complete the Ant, Butterfly, and Grasshopper Mini-book on pp. 33-35 from *Biology for the Grammar Stage Lapbooking Templates*. Cut out the mini-book and color the picture. Have the students tell you what they have learned about the ant, butterfly, and grasshopper. Then, write their favorite piece of information inside the mini-book and glue it into the lapbook.

Vocabulary

The following definition is a guide; the students' definitions do not need to match word for word.

- **Insect** – An invertebrate animal that has three body parts (head, thorax, and abdomen) and six legs. (SW pg. 94)

Multi-week Projects and Activities

Unit Project

- **Animal Diet Chart** – Add the ant, butterfly, and grasshopper to the Animal Diet Chart on SW pp. 6-7; pictures for this project are on SW pg. 109. The placement chart for this project can be found in the Appendix on pg. 178.
- **(Optional) Habitat Posters** – This week, add the ant, butterfly, and grasshopper to the students' habitat posters. The placement chart for this project can be found in the Appendix on pg. 179.

Projects for this Week

- **Coloring Pages** – You can have the students color the following pages from *Biology for the Grammar Stage Coloring Pages*: Ant pg. 64, Butterfly pg. 65, Grasshopper pg. 66.
- **Field Trip** – Take the students to visit a zoo this week. While there, have them observe the animals and choose several on which to fill out an Animal Observation Sheet. This sheet can be found in the Appendix of this guide on pg. 187.
- **Ant** – Build your own ant farm using the directions from the following website:
  - http://tlc.howstuffworks.com/family/ant-activities1.htm

- ✂ **Butterfly** – Have the students make a poster depicting the life cycle of a butterfly. You can use the cards provided for you in the Appendix on pg. 191 of this guide or have the students draw their own.
- ✂ **Grasshopper** – Have the students make grasshopper clothespin. Begin by painting a clothespin completely green. While it dries, cut a green pipe cleaner into 4 sections and repeat so that you have 8 sections. Curl the ends of two of the sections for antennae and bend the remaining 6 sections for legs. Once the clothespin is dry, attach the legs and antennae. Finally, add two googly eyes just below the antennae to complete your grasshopper.

Memorization

- Continue to work on memorizing the *Characteristics of Invertebrates* poem. (SW pg. 101)

<u>Characteristics of Invertebrates</u>
Invertebrates have no backbone
They live worldwide, in every zone
Ninety-seven percent of animals are in this group
Like the clams and shrimp that end up in your soup

Quiz

Weekly Quiz

- "Animal Week 20 Quiz" on SW pg. Q-24.

Quiz Answers

1. 3, 6
2. True
3. False (*Caterpillars turn into butterflies through metamorphosis.*)
4. True
5. Answers will vary

Notes

Possible Schedules for Week 20

Two Days a Week Schedule	
Day 1	**Day 2**
❑ Read about Insects and Butterflies ❑ Add information about the butterfly to the students' Narration Page ❑ Do the Scientific Demonstration: Butterfly Glider ❑ Work on memorizing the *Characteristics of Invertebrates* Poem ❑ Define insect	❑ Read about the Ant and Grasshopper ❑ Complete the students' Narration Page ❑ Add this week's animals to the Animal Diet Chart (or the Habitat Posters) ❑ Take the Animal Week 20 quiz ❑ Choose one of the projects from the week to complete

Five Days a Week Schedule				
Day 1	**Day 2**	**Day 3**	**Day 4**	**Day 5**
❑ Read about Insects and Ants ❑ Add information about the ant to the students' Narration Page ❑ Do the Ant Project	❑ Read about the Butterfly ❑ Add information about the butterfly to the students' Narration Page ❑ Do the Butterfly Project	❑ Do the Scientific Demonstration: Butterfly Glider ❑ Define insect	❑ Read about the Grasshopper ❑ Add information about the grasshopper to the students' Narration Page ❑ Do the Grasshopper Project	❑ Take the Animal Week 20 quiz ❑ Add this week's animals to the Animal Diet Chart (or the Habitat Posters)
All Week Long ❑ Work on memorizing the *Characteristics of Invertebrates* Poem				

Biology for the Grammar Stage

Human Body Unit

Human Body Unit Overview
(10 weeks)

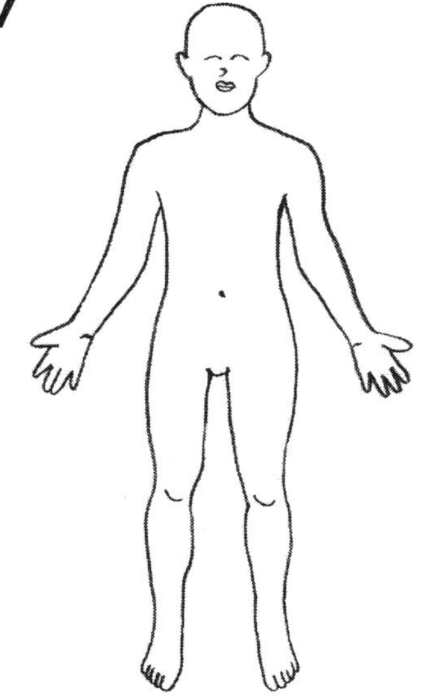

Books Scheduled

Encyclopedias

- *DK First Human Body Encyclopedia*

  OR

- *Kingfisher Science Encyclopedia*

Scientific Demonstration Book

- *Janice VanCleave's Biology for Every Kid*

Sequence for Study

- **Week 1:** Basic Building Blocks
- **Week 2:** The Skeletal System
- **Week 3:** The Muscular System
- **Week 4:** The Nervous System
- **Week 5:** The Five Senses
- **Week 6:** The Circulatory System
- **Week 7:** The Respiratory System
- **Week 8:** The Digestive System
- **Week 9:** The Urinary System (plus Genes)
- **Week 10:** The Immune System

Human Body Poem to Memorize

The Systems of the Human Body

The skeletal system
Holds me upright

The muscular system
Moves me all night

The nervous system
Sends cells a note

The circulatory system
Keeps blood afloat

The respiratory system
Breathes in and out

The digestive system
Breaks down the trout

The urinary system
Could fill a moat

The immune system
Fixes strep throat

Supplies Needed for the Unit

Week	Supplies needed
1	Pencil, Clear tape, Magnifying glass
2	1 Raw chicken bone, 1 Jar with lid, White vinegar
3	Items of varying weights, like a paper clip, toothbrush, glass, can, book
4	A large book or something else that will make a loud noise, Cotton balls (or rolled-up paper towels), See-through barrier (a wire screen, plastic or glass window)
5	Mirror, Toothpicks, Blindfold, Clothespin, Apple, Onion, Pencils, Masking tape
6	Modeling clay, Paper, Match
7	Plastic dishpan, 2 Feet of aquarium tubing, 1 Gallon milk jug, Masking tape, Pens
8	Paper towels, Slender glass jar, Masking tape, Marking pen
9	Family pictures
10	Milk, Measuring cup, 2 Pint Jars

Unit Vocabulary

1. **Cell** – A tiny, living unit that is the building block of all living things.
2. **Skeleton** – The framework of 206 bones that supports your body; it allows you to move and protects certain organs.
3. **Muscle** – A type of tissue that makes the bones of your body move and that is controlled by your brain.
4. **Neuron** – A nerve cell that makes up the nervous system and carries electrical messages throughout the body.
5. **Senses** – The ability of the body to take in and respond to information from its surroundings.
6. **Blood vessel** – A tube that carries blood through the body.
7. **Alveoli** – Tiny air bags found in your lungs.
8. **Digestion** – The process by which your food is broken down.
9. **Kidney** – The organ in the body responsible for removing waste from itself and regulating the body's fluid levels.
10. **Bacteria** – A group of microscopic organisms that can cause diseases.

Week 1: Basic Building Blocks Lesson Plans

Scientific Demonstration: Fingerprints

Supplies Needed

- ✓ Pencil
- ✓ Clear tape
- ✓ Magnifying glass

Purpose

This demonstration is meant to help the students to observe the patterns in their fingerprints.

Instructions and Explanation

The instructions and explanation for this scientific demonstration are found on pp. 176-177 of *Janice VanCleave's Biology for Every Kid*. Have the students complete the Lab Report on SW pg. 53. (**Note** — *Have the students paste their fingerprints on the Lab Report Sheet instead of on a separate sheet of paper.*)

Take it Further

Have the students use paint and their fingers to create fingerprint animals and flowers.

Science-Oriented Books

Reading Assignments

- 📖 *DK First Human Body Encyclopedia pp. 4-5 (Amazing Body), pp. 8-9 (Building Blocks), pp. 68-69 (All Wrapped Up)*
- 📖 *Kingfisher Science Encyclopedia pp. 98-99 (Body Organization), pp. 100-101 (Skin, Hair, and Nails)*

(Optional) Additional topics to explore this week: Organization of the Body, At your fingertips *(from the DK First Human Body Encyclopedia)*

Discussion Questions

After reading the selected pages from the encyclopedias, ask the following questions in your discussion time:

Cells

- **?** What are cells?
- **?** How many cells do we have in our body?

Skin

- **?** What are the two layers of the skin?
- **?** What is the job of the skin?

Hair

- **?** Where can hair be found on the human body?

? Does it always look the same?

(Optional) Additional Books

- *BodyWorks - Skin and Hair* by Katherine Goode
- *Your Skin and Mine: Revised Edition (Let's-Read-and-Find... Science 2)* by Paul Showers

Notebooking

Writing Assignments

- **Narration Page** – Have the students dictate, copy, or write one to four sentences for cells, skin, and hair on SW pg. 52. They can include information that they find interesting on each topic or material that you would like them to remember. For example, this week, the students could dictate, copy, or write the following for the cells:

  Cells are the building blocks of our body.
  We have billions of them.

- **(Optional) Lapbook** – Complete the Cell and Skin Mini-book on pp. 38-39 from *Biology for the Grammar Stage Lapbooking Templates*. For each one, cut out the mini-book and color the picture. Have the students tell you what they have learned about cells or skin and write it for them on the inside of the mini-book. Then, glue the mini-book into the lapbook.

Vocabulary

The following definition is a guide. The students' definitions do not need to match word for word.

- **Cell** – A tiny, living unit that is the building block of all living things. (SW pg. 91)

Multi-week Projects and Activities

Unit Project

- **Human Body Project** – Each week, the students will paste the parts of the body that you are learning about onto the body outline. Add each part at the end of the week while doing an oral review of what you have learned by asking, "Do you remember what this part does?". This project will continue through week 9. This week, have the students add hair to the body outline on SW pp. 50-51. (**Optional** — *You could also make a life size version of this project. This week, trace your child's body and add hair to the wall-sized version of their body.*)
- **(Optional) Microscope Work** – Purchase a prepared slide of skin and hair cells or pull one of your own hairs to look at under your microscope. Complete a microscope worksheet found on pg. 192 of the Appendix. If you do not own a microscope, you can view these cells at the following websites:
  - **Skin** – http://www.dmscocamera.com/cell.asp?did=69&id=9
  - **Hair** – http://blog.microscopeworld.com/2009/07/hair-under-microscope.html

Projects for this Week

- ✂ **Coloring Pages –** You can have the students color the following pages from *Biology for the Grammar Stage Coloring Pages*: Cell pg. 67, Skin pg. 68, Hair pg. 69 (***Note:** Have the student draw hair on the body found on this coloring page.*)
- ✂ **Body Organization –** Have the students create a poster that shows the organization of the body (e.g. cells form tissue, tissue forms organs, organs form systems, systems work together to keep the body functioning). You can use the Body Organization Cards found in the Appendix of the guide on pg. 193.
- ✂ **Cell –** Have the students make a Jell-O replica of a cell. Use a margarine container for your cell membrane, Jell-O for cytoplasm. Prepare the Jell-O according to the package directions. Fill your container three-quarters of the way with the mixture and place it in the fridge until it is soft set (about 30 minutes). Then, insert a grape in the center for the nucleus of the cell and use your imagination for materials for the remaining organelles.
- ✂ **Hair –** Have the students compare their hair with the hair of others in their family or group. You will need paper, tape, and several students or family members for this activity. Pull a hair from each person and tape each of them on a sheet of paper. Mark each one with a number and record the person's name with that number on a separate sheet of paper. Then, have each of the students guess at whose hair belongs to who.

Memorization

This week, read over *The Systems of the Human Body* poem several times with the students. (SW pg. 102)

<u>The Systems of the Human Body</u>

The skeletal system
Holds me upright

The muscular system
Moves me all night

The nervous system
Sends cells a note

The circulatory system
Keeps blood afloat

The respiratory system
Breathes in and out

The digestive system
Breaks down the trout

The urinary system
Could fill a moat

The immune system
Fixes strep throat

Quiz

Weekly Quiz

- "Human Body Unit Week 1 Quiz" on SW pg. Q-25.

Quiz Answers

1. Billions
2. Dermis, Epidermis
3. False (*Hair is made up of dead cells.*)
4. Answers will vary

Possible Schedules for Week 1

Two Days a Week Schedule	
Day 1	**Day 2**
❑ Read Amazing Body and Building Blocks (or Body Organization) ❑ Add information about cells to the students' Narration Page ❑ Do the Scientific Demonstration: Fingerprints ❑ Work on memorizing *The Systems of the Human Body* poem	❑ Read All Wrapped up (or Skin, Hair, Nails) ❑ Complete the Narration Page for this week ❑ Define cell ❑ Begin working on the Human Body Project ❑ Take the Human Body Week 1 quiz

Five Days a Week Schedule				
Day 1	**Day 2**	**Day 3**	**Day 4**	**Day 5**
❑ Read Building Blocks (or Body Organization) ❑ Add information about cells to the students' Narration Page ❑ Do the Cell Project	❑ Read Amazing Body ❑ Do the Body Organization Project ❑ Begin working on the Human Body Project	❑ Read All Wrapped up (or Skin, Hair, and Nails) ❑ Add information about the skin and hair to the students' Narration Page ❑ Do the Hair Project	❑ Do the Scientific Demonstration: Fingerprints ❑ Define cell	❑ Take the Human Body Week 1 quiz ❑ Do the optional microscope work
All Week Long ❑ Work on memorizing *The Systems of the Human Body* poem				

Notes

Week 2: Skeletal System Lesson Plans

Scientific Demonstration: Soft Bones

Supplies Needed

- ✓ 1 Raw chicken bone
- ✓ 1 Jar with a lid
- ✓ White vinegar

Purpose

This demonstration is meant to help the students to observe that bones can become flexible once the minerals are removed.

Instructions and Explanation

The instructions and explanation for this scientific demonstration are found on pp. 184-185 of *Janice VanCleave's Biology for Every Kid*. Have the students complete the Lab Report on SW pg. 55.

Take it Further

Have the students examine and observe the bones in a chicken skeleton, including the neck. Discuss with them the importance of bones and what they do for the chicken.

Science-Oriented Books

Reading Assignments

- *DK First Human Body Encyclopedia pp. 12-13 (Skeleton), pp. 16-17 (Bendable Backbone), pp. 14-15 (Head Case), pp. 20-21 (Bones and Cartilage)*
- *Kingfisher Science Encyclopedia pp. 102-103 (The Skeleton), pg. 104 (Bones)*

(Optional) Additional topic to explore this week: Living Bone *(from the DK First Human Body Encyclopedia)*

Discussion Questions

After reading the selected pages from the encyclopedias, ask the following questions in your discussion time:

Skeleton

- ? What is the job of the skeleton?
- ? Does the skeleton change as we grow up?

Skull

- ? What does the skull protect?
- ? What else does the skull do?

Bones

- ? What do the bones do for the body?
- ? What are bones made of?

(Optional) Additional Books

- *The Skeleton Inside You (Let's-Read-and-Find... Science 2)* by Philip Balestrino
- *Bones: Skeletons and How They Work* by Steve Jenkins
- *A Book about Your Skeleton (Hello Reader!)* by Ruth Belov Gross

Notebooking

Writing Assignments

- **Narration Page** – Have the students dictate, copy, or write one to four sentences for the skeleton, skull, and bones on SW pg. 54. They can include information that they find interesting on each topic or material that you would like them to remember. (*See the Human Body Week 1 for a sample.*)
- **(Optional) Lapbook** – Complete the Skeletal System Tab-book on pg. 40 from *Biology for the Grammar Stage Lapbooking Templates*. Have the students cut out the pages and color the cover. Then, have them tell you the purpose (or job) of the skeletal system and record it on the purpose page. After that, have the students tell you what they have learned about bones and the skull. Write it for them on the respective pages. Finally, staple the pages together and glue the tab-book into the lapbook.

Vocabulary

The following definition is a guide. The students' definitions do not need to match word for word.

- **Skeleton** – The framework of 206 bones that supports your body; it allows you to move and protects certain organs. (SW pg. 97)

Multi-week Projects and Activities

Unit Project

- **Human Body Project** – This week, have the students add the skeleton to the back of the body outline on SW pp. 50-51; pictures for this project are on SW pg. 111. As you add the part, do a quick oral review of the skeletal system by asking, "Do you remember what the skeleton does?". (**Optional** — *You could also make a life size version of this project. This week, blow up the included skeleton picture to wall size or have the students draw an outline of a skeleton on their body outline.*)
- **(Optional) Microscope Work** – Purchase a prepared slide of bone cells to look at under your microscope. Complete a microscope worksheet found on pg. 192 of the Appendix. If you do not own a microscope, you can view bone cells at the following website:
  - http://physioweb.org/skeletal/bone_tissue.html

Projects for this Week

- **Coloring Pages** – You can have the students color the following pages from *Biology for* *the Grammar Stage Coloring Pages*: Skeleton pg. 70, Skull pg. 71, Bones pg. 72.

- ✂ **Skeleton –** Have the students make a model of the backbone. You will need 5 to 6 spools of thread, 2 cardboard discs and some string for this project. Tie one end of one of the cardboard discs to the string, then thread the string through the center of the spools of thread. Now tie the remaining cardboard discs to the other end of the string, close to the top of the last spool of thread. You now have a model of the spine that will twist and bend in all directions, just like our backbone.
- ✂ **Skull –** Have the students make a model of the skull. You will need two water balloons per student and protective materials (such as fabric, bubble wrap and cardboard). Fill both balloons with water. Then, have the students cover one of their balloons with their choice of protective material to create a "skull" for their balloon brain. Once they are done, have them take their balloons outside and throw both of them against the wall. Did their "skull" protect their balloon brain?
- ✂ **Bones –** Have the students examine a bone up close. You will need a raw chicken leg bone, gloves, magnifying glass, and a sharp knife. Have the students observe the bone with the magnifying glass, noting the shape, color, and feel of the bone. Then, carefully cut the bone in half. (**Caution** — *Only adults should cut the bone!*) Have the students observe the inside of the bone, noting the similarities and differences between the outside and inside of the bone. Discuss with the students the different layers of the bone and what they do.

Memorization

This week, work on memorizing the following lines from *The Systems of the Human Body* poem. (SW pg. 102)

<u>The Systems of the Human Body</u>
The skeletal system
Holds me upright

Quiz

Weekly Quiz

- "Human Body Unit Week 2 Quiz" on SW pg. Q-26.

Quiz Answers

1. Supports your body, Allows you to move, Protects certain organs
2. Brain
3. True
4. Answers will vary

Possible Schedules for Week 2

Two Days a Week Schedule	
Day 1	**Day 2**
❑ Read Bones and Cartilage (or Bones) ❑ Add information about bones to the students' Narration Page ❑ Do the Scientific Demonstration: Soft Bones ❑ Work on memorizing the *Human Body* poem	❑ Read Skeleton, Bendable Backbone, and Head Case (or The Skeleton) ❑ Complete the Narration Page for this week ❑ Define skeleton ❑ Add to the Human Body Project ❑ Take the Human Body Week 2 quiz

Five Days a Week Schedule				
Day 1	**Day 2**	**Day 3**	**Day 4**	**Day 5**
❑ Read Skeleton and Bendable Backbone (or The Skeleton) ❑ Add information about the skeleton to the students' Narration Page ❑ Do the Skeleton Project	❑ Read Head Case ❑ Add information about the skull to the students' Narration Page ❑ Do the Skull Project ❑ Add to the Human Body Project	❑ Read Bones and Cartilage (or Bones) ❑ Add information about the bones to the students' Narration Page ❑ Do the Bones Project	❑ Do the Scientific Demonstration: Soft Bones ❑ Define skeleton	❑ Take the Human Body Week 2 quiz ❑ Do the optional microscope work
All Week Long ❑ Work on memorizing the *Human Body* poem				

Notes

Week 3: Muscular System Lesson Plans

Scientific Demonstration: Muscle Strength

Supplies Needed

✓ Items of various weights, such as a paper clip, toothbrush, glass, a can, a book

Purpose

This demonstration is meant to help the students to see how objects of varying weight affect how their muscles work.

Instructions

1. Have the students choose 5 items of varying weights and lay them in a line on a table in front of them.
2. Have them pick up each object and note the muscle power it takes to pick up each on the chart on the Lab Report on SW pg. 57.
3. Once the students have picked up each of the objects, have them rate each as light, medium or heavy on the chart on their Lab Report.
4. Have the students complete their Lab Report.

Explanation

This demonstration was designed to help the students understand how their muscles work. They should have seen that the heavier the object, the more muscle power it took to pick it up.

Take it Further

Have the students use a scale to weigh each of the objects to see how accurate their predictions were.

Science-Oriented Books

Reading Assignments

- *DK First Human Body Encyclopedia pp. 22-23 (Moving Joints), pp. 24-25 (The Body's Muscles), pp. 26-27 (How Muscles Work)*
- *Kingfisher Science Encyclopedia pg. 105 (Joints), pp. 106-107 (Muscles and Movement)*

(Optional) Additional topic to explore this week: Body Language *(from the DK First Human Body Encyclopedia)*

Discussion Questions

After reading the selected pages from the encyclopedias, ask the following questions in your discussion time:

Joints

? What are the jobs of the joints?

? Where are the joints located in the body?

Muscles

? What are the jobs of the muscles?

? What are the three types of muscles?

How Muscles Work

? How do muscles work?

(Optional) Additional Books

- *Bend and Stretch: Learning About Your Bones and Muscles (Amazing Body)* by Pamela Hill Nettleton
- *Your Muscles (Your Body) by Anne Ylvisaker The Mighty Muscular-Skeletal System: How Do My Bones and Muscles Work?* by John Burstein
- *Your Muscles (Your Body)* by Anne Ylvisaker

Notebooking

Writing Assignments

- ☐ **Narration Page –** Have the students dictate, copy, or write one to four sentences for the joints, muscles, and how muscles work on SW pg. 56. They can include information that they find interesting on each topic or material that you would like them to remember. (*See the Human Body Week 1 for a sample.*)

- ☐ **(Optional) Lapbook –** Complete the Muscular System Tab-book on pg. 41 from *Biology for the Grammar Stage Lapbooking Templates*. Have the students cut out the pages and color the cover. Then, have them tell you the purpose (or job) of the muscular system and record it on the purpose page. After that, have the students tell you what they have learned about muscles and how muscles work. Write it for them on the respective pages. Finally, staple the pages together and glue the tab-book into the lapbook.

Vocabulary

The following definition is a guide. The students' definitions do not need to match word for word.

- **Muscle –** A type of tissue that makes the bones of your body move and that is controlled by your brain. (SW pg. 95)

Multi-week Projects and Activities

Unit Project

- **Human Body Project –** This week, have the students add the arm muscle to the front of the body outline on SW pp. 50-51; pictures for this project are on SW pg. 111. As you add the part, do a quick oral review of the muscular system by asking, "Do you remember what the muscles do for the body?". (**Optional** — *You could also make a life size version of this project. This week, blow up the included arm muscle picture to wall size or have the students draw several muscles on their body outline.*)
- **(Optional) Microscope Work –** Purchase a prepared slide of muscle cells to look at under your microscope. Complete a microscope worksheet found on pg. 192 of the Appendix. If you do not own a microscope, you can view bone cells at the following

website:
- https://ehumanbiofield.wikispaces.com/Muscular+system+EP

Projects for this Week

- **Coloring Pages** – You can have the students color the following pages from *Biology for the Grammar Stage Coloring Pages*: Joints pg. 73, Muscles pg. 74.
- **Joints** – Have the students make a model of a pivot, hinge, and ball and socket joint. You will need a brad, card stock, scissors, and a hole punch to make a pivot joint. You will need two lengths of 1x2 boards, a hinge, a screwdriver, and several screws to make a hinge joint. You will need one length of ½" plastic pipe, one length of ¾" plastic pipe, one ½" plastic pipe tee, one ¾" plastic pipe tee, a pipe saw, and two rubber bands to make a ball and socket joint. See the Appendix pg. 194 for directions for this project.
- **Muscles** – There are three main types of muscles — smooth, cardiac, and skeletal. Have the students research these three types of muscles and share what they have learned (i.e. the similarities and differences).
- **How Muscles Work** – Muscles can work in pairs to help move the body. One of those pairs includes the biceps and triceps muscles. Have the students place their hands on the front of their arm and bend their hand toward their shoulder and then extend their arm. Then, have them place their hand on the back of their arm and bend their hand toward their shoulder one more time. Did they notice anything moving? (*The students should feel a bulge in the front of their arm from the biceps muscle when it bends up and at the back of their arm from the triceps muscle when they extend it out.*)

Memorization

- This week, add the following lines from *The Systems of the Human Body* poem. (SW pg. 102)

  The Systems of the Human Body

  The muscular system
  Moves me all night

Quiz

Weekly Quiz

- "Human Body Unit Week 3 Quiz" on SW pg. Q-27.

Quiz Answers

1. Brain
2. Contract
3. True
4. Answers will vary

Possible Schedules for Week 3

Two Days a Week Schedule	
Day 1	**Day 2**
❑ Read The Body's Muscles (or Muscles and Movement) ❑ Add information about the muscles to the students' Narration Page ❑ Do the Scientific Demonstration: Muscle Strength ❑ Work on memorizing *The Systems of the Human Body* poem	❑ Read Moving Joints and How Muscles Work (or Joints) ❑ Complete the Narration Page for this week ❑ Define muscles ❑ Add to the Human Body Project ❑ Take the Human Body Week 3 quiz

Five Days a Week Schedule				
Day 1	**Day 2**	**Day 3**	**Day 4**	**Day 5**
❑ Read Moving Joints (or Joints) ❑ Add information about the joints to the students' Narration Page ❑ Do the Joints Project	❑ Read The Body's Muscles ❑ Add information about the muscles to the students' Narration Page ❑ Do the Muscles Project	❑ Read How Muscles Work (or Muscles and Movement) ❑ Add information about how muscles work to the students' Narration Page ❑ Do the How Muscles Work Project	❑ Do the Scientific Demonstration: Muscle Strength ❑ Define muscles ❑ Add to the Human Body Project	❑ Take the Human Body Week 3 quiz ❑ Do the optional microscope work
All Week Long ❑ Work on memorizing *The Systems of the Human Body* poem				

Notes

Week 4: Nervous System Lesson Plans

Scientific Demonstration: Reflexes

Supplies Needed

- ✓ A large book or something else that will make a loud noise
- ✓ Cotton balls (or rolled-up paper towels)
- ✓ A see-through barrier (a wire screen, plastic or glass window)

Purpose

This demonstration is meant to help the students to learn about reflexes.

Instructions

1. First, test the students reflex reaction to loud noises. Begin by suddenly slamming a book on a table to create a loud noise. The students should have done one of these — twitched, moved their heads, blinked their eyes, put their hands up, or screamed.
2. Then, test the students' blink reflex. Have the students stand place a see-through barrier, like a piece of glass, plastic, or wire screen in front of their face. Throw a cotton ball at them. Did they blink?
3. Have the students complete their Lab Report on SW pg. 59.

Explanation

Reflexes are used to protect the body without us having to think about what is happening. They get us away from objects that might hurt us, before they hurt us. For example, if you put your hand on a hot stove, you immediately remove your hand BEFORE the message, "Hey, my hand is on a hot, burning stove!" gets to your brain. Our built-in reflexes are designed to protect us.

Take it Further

The knee jerk reflex is one we are all familiar with. The doctor hits your knee and your leg kicks out. Try it out with the students by having them sit with their legs bent on a high chair or table so that their legs can swing freely. Hit their leg just below the knee with the side of your hand. (*If you hit the right place, the students' legs will kick out immediately.*)

Science-Oriented Books

Reading Assignments

- 🕮 *DK First Human Body Encyclopedia pp. 30-31 (Headquarters), pp. 32-33 (Network of Nerves), pp. 108-109 (Sleep)*
- 🕮 *Kingfisher Science Encyclopedia pp. 108-109 (The Brain and Nervous System), pg. 110 (Sleep)*

(Optional) Additional topics to explore this week: Look Out, Balancing Act *(from the DK First Human Body Encyclopedia)*

Discussion Questions

After reading the selected pages from the encyclopedias, ask the following questions in your discussion time:

Brain

- ? What is the job of the brain?
- ? What are the six main parts of the brain?

Nervous System

- ? What is the job of the nervous system?
- ? What is the nervous system composed of?

Sleep

- ? Why does the body need sleep?

(Optional) Additional Books

- *The Nervous System (New True Books: Health)* by Christine Taylor-Butler
- *The Brain: Our Nervous System* by Seymour Simon
- *Brain, Nerves, and Senses (Understanding the Human Body)* by Steve Parker
- *You've Got Nerve!: The Secrets of the Brain and Nerves (The Gross and Goofy Body)* by Melissa Stewart

Notebooking

Writing Assignments

- **Narration Page** – Have the students dictate, copy, or write one to four sentences for the brain, nervous system, and sleep on SW pg. 58. They can include information that they find interesting on each topic or material that you would like them to remember. (*See the Human Body Week 1 for a sample.*)

- **(Optional) Lapbook** – Complete the Nervous System Tab-book on pg. 42 from *Biology for the Grammar Stage Lapbooking Templates*. Have the students cut out the pages and color the cover. Then, have them tell you the purpose (or job) of the nervous system and record it on the purpose page. After that, have the students tell you what they have learned about the brain and spinal cord. Write it for them on the respective pages. Finally, staple the pages together and glue the tab-book into the lapbook.

Vocabulary

The following definition is a guide. The students' definitions do not need to match word for word.

- **Neuron** – A nerve cell that makes up the nervous system and carries electrical messages throughout the body. (SW pg. 96)

Multi-week Projects and Activities

Unit Project

- **Human Body Project** – This week, have the students add the brain to the front of the body outline and the spinal cord to the back of the body outline on SW pp. 50-51; pictures for this project are on SW pg. 111. As you add the part, do a quick oral review of the nervous system by asking, "Do you remember what the brain and spinal cord do?".

(**Optional** — *You could also make a life size version of this project. This week, blow up the included brain picture to wall size or have the students draw the brain on their body outline.*)

- ✂ **(Optional) Microscope Work –** Purchase a prepared slide of brain cells to look at under your microscope. Complete a microscope worksheet found on pg. 192 of the Appendix. If you do not own a microscope, you can view brain cells at the following website:
  - http://www.braindamage.net/ *(You will need to scroll down to see the images. There are three pictures that give a good comparison between healthy and damaged brain tissue.)*

Projects for this Week

- ✂ **Coloring Pages –** You can have the students color the following pages from *Biology for the Grammar Stage Coloring Pages*: Brain pg. 75, Nervous System pg. 76, Sleep pg. 77.
- ✂ **Brain –** Test the students short term memory. Choose seven to ten of the terms that you have studied so far. Then, lay out the animal pictures from the SW on pp. 101 and 103 picture side up in a row on the table. Tell the students they have one minute to memorize all of the animals in the correct order. After one minute take the cards away and have the students tell you or write down what they remember.
- ✂ **Nervous System –** Have the students make a model of a neuron. You can use different colors of modeling clay to make the different parts of the nerve cell. You can use the diagram from the encyclopedia you used as a visual example.
- ✂ **Sleep –** Have the students record one of their dreams. They can dictate the dream to you as you write it down on a sheet of paper. Then, let the students illustrate the page.

Memorization

This week, add the following lines from *The Systems of the Human Body* poem. (SW pg. 102)

<u>The Systems of the Human Body</u>

The nervous system
Sends cells a note

Quiz

Weekly Quiz

- "Human Body Unit Week 4 Quiz" on SW pg. Q-28.

Quiz Answers

1. Neuron
2. False (*The brain is the command center for the nervous system.*)
3. True
4. Answers will vary

Possible Schedules for Week 4

Two Days a Week Schedule	
Day 1	**Day 2**
❑ Read Network of Nerves (or The Brain and Nervous System) ❑ Add information about the nervous system to the students' Narration Page ❑ Do the Scientific Demonstration: Reflexes ❑ Work on memorizing *The Systems of the Human Body* poem	❑ Read Headquarters and Sleep ❑ Complete the Narration Page for this week ❑ Define neuron ❑ Add to the Human Body Project ❑ Take the Human Body Week 4 quiz

Five Days a Week Schedule				
Day 1	**Day 2**	**Day 3**	**Day 4**	**Day 5**
❑ Read Brain (or The Brain and Nervous System) ❑ Add information about the brain to the students' Narration Page ❑ Do the Brain Project	❑ Read Network of Nerves ❑ Add information about the nervous system to the students' Narration Page ❑ Do the Nervous System Project	❑ Do the Scientific Demonstration: Reflexes ❑ Define neuron ❑ Add to the Human Body Project	❑ Read Sleep ❑ Add information about sleep to the students' Narration Page ❑ Do the Sleep Project	❑ Take the Human Body Week 4 quiz ❑ Do the optional microscope work
All Week Long ❑ Work on memorizing *The Systems of the Human Body* poem				

Notes

Week 5: The Five Senses Lesson Plans

Scientific Demonstration: Testing the Senses

Supplies Needed

- ✓ Hand mirror
- ✓ Toothpicks
- ✓ Blindfold
- ✓ Clothespin
- ✓ Apple
- ✓ Onion
- ✓ Two sharpened pencils
- ✓ Masking tape

Purpose

These demonstrations are meant to help the students to learn more about their senses.

Instructions and Explanation

This week is a bit different than any other in this program. Instead of having one demonstration for the week, you will have four. Instead of completing a lab report for each one, the students will just add what they have learned about the senses on the narration sheets on SW pp. 60-61.

- **Sight –** Do the "Big and Little" demonstration that looks at the effect light has on the pupil. The instructions and explanation for this scientific demonstration are found on pp. 156-157 of *Janice VanCleave's Biology for Every Kid.*
- **Hearing –** Do the "Sound and Direction" demonstration which tests the students' ability to observe the direction of a sound source. The instructions and explanation for this scientific demonstration are found on pp. 170-171 of *Janice VanCleave's Biology for Every Kid.*
- **Smell and Taste –** Do the "Have an Onion" demonstration which examines the students' sensitivity to taste. The instructions and explanation for this scientific demonstration are found on pp. 150-151 of *Janice VanCleave's Biology for Every Kid.*
- **Touch –** Do the "How Do You Feel" demonstration which analyzes the sensitivity of different parts of the students' skin. The instructions and explanation for this scientific demonstration are found on pp. 196-197 of *Janice VanCleave's Biology for Every Kid.*

Science-Oriented Books

Reading Assignments

- *DK First Human Body Encyclopedia pp. 38-39 (How we see), pp. 44-45 (Listen Up), pp. 36-37 (Taste and Smell), pp. 34-35 (Touchy Feely)*
- *Kingfisher Science Encyclopedia pg. 112 (Touch), pg. 113 (Taste and Smell), pg. 114-115*

(Eyes and Seeing), pp. 116-117 (Ears, Hearing and Balance)

(Optional) Coordinating topic to study this week: Eye to the Brain *(from the DK First Human Body Encyclopedia)*

Discussion Questions

After reading the selected pages from the encyclopedias, ask the following questions for each of the senses in your discussion time:

- ? What does the _________ sense do for the body?
- ? What part of the body is responsible for the _________ sense?

(Optional) Additional Books

- *Look, Listen, Taste, Touch, and Smell: Learning About Your Five Senses (Amazing Body)* by Pamela Hill Nettleton
- *My Five Senses Big Book (Let's-Read-And-Find...* by Margaret Miller and Aliki
- *The Magic School Bus Explores the Senses* by Joanna Cole
- *The Listening Walk* by Paul Showers

Notebooking

Writing Assignments

- ☐ **Narration Page** – Have the students dictate, copy, or write one to four sentences for each of the senses on SW pp. 60-61. They can include information that they find interesting on each topic or material that you would like them to remember. (*See the Human Body Week 1 for a sample.*)

- ☐ **(Optional) Lapbook** – Work on Five Senses Accordion Fold-book on pg. 43 from *Biology for the Grammar Stage Lapbooking Templates*. Color each of the five senses pictures on the fold-book. Have the students tell you what they have learned about each of the senses. Then, write for them their favorite piece of information on the fold-book. Finally, fold the book like an accordion and glue the back into the lapbook.

Vocabulary

The following definition is a guide. The students' definitions do not need to match word for word.

- **Senses** – The ability of the body to take in and respond to information from its surroundings. (SW pg. 97)

Multi-week Projects and Activities

Unit Project

- There is nothing to add to the unit project this week.

Projects for this Week

- **Coloring Pages** – You can have the students color the following pages from *Biology for the Grammar Stage Coloring Pages*: The Five Senses pg. 78.

Memorization

- Review the following lines from *The Systems of the Human Body* poem. (SW pg. 102)

  <u>The Systems of the Human Body</u>

  The skeletal system
  Holds me upright

  The muscular system
  Moves me all night

  The nervous system
  Sends cells a note

Quiz

Weekly Quiz

- "Human Body Unit Week 5 Quiz" on SW pg. Q-29.

Quiz Answers

1. Nose-smell, Ear-hearing, Eye-sight, Skin-feel, Tongue-taste
2. True
3. Answers will vary

Notes

Possible Schedules for Week 5

Two Days a Week Schedule	
Day 1	**Day 2**
❑ Read about How we See and Listen Up (or Eyes and Seeing; Ears, Hearing and Balance) ❑ Add information about sight and hearing to the students' Narration Page ❑ Do the Scientific Demonstrations for sight and hearing ❑ Work on memorizing *The Systems of the Human Body* poem	❑ Read about Taste and Smell and Touchy Feely (or Touch, Taste and Smell) ❑ Complete the students' Narration Page ❑ Do the Scientific Demonstrations for touch, smell and taste ❑ Define senses ❑ Take the Human Body Week 5 quiz

Five Days a Week Schedule				
Day 1	**Day 2**	**Day 3**	**Day 4**	**Day 5**
❑ Read about How we See (or Eyes and Seeing) ❑ Add information about sight to the students' Narration Page ❑ Do the Scientific Demonstration for sight	❑ Read about Listen Up (or Ears, Hearing and Balance) ❑ Add information about hearing to the students' Narration Page ❑ Do the Scientific Demonstration for hearing	❑ Read about Taste and Smell ❑ Add information about taste and smell to the students' Narration Page ❑ Do the Scientific Demonstration for taste and smell	❑ Read about Touchy Feely (or Touch) ❑ Add information about touch to the students' Narration Page ❑ Do the Scientific Demonstration for touch	❑ Define senses ❑ Take the Human Body Week 5 quiz
All Week Long ❑ Work on memorizing *The Systems of the Human Body* poem				

Week 6: The Circulatory System Lesson Plans

Scientific Demonstration: Heartbeat

Supplies Needed

- ✓ Modeling clay
- ✓ Paper
- ✓ Match

Purpose

This demonstration is meant to help the students to observe the vibrations created by their pulse.

Instructions and Explanation

The instructions and explanation for this scientific demonstration are found on pp. 188-189 of *Janice VanCleave's Biology for Every Kid*. Have the students complete the Lab Report on SW pg. 63.

Take it Further

Have the students measure their pulses at their wrists and necks. Here's how:

- ALWAYS use two fingers to check your pulse. NEVER use your thumb as one of those fingers!
- To find the radial pulse, which is just inside of the wrist, place your fingers at the base of your thumb on the inside of your wrist and feel the beating.
- To find the carotid pulse, which is on the side of the neck, place your two fingers between your windpipe and the large neck muscle. Press lightly until you feel the beating.

Science-Oriented Books

Reading Assignments

- *DK First Human Body Encyclopedia pp. 50-51 (Boom, Boom), pp. 48-49 (Blood Flow), pp. 54-55 (Blood Cells)*
- *Kingfisher Science Encyclopedia pp. 120-121 (Heart and Circulation), pg. 122 (Blood)*

(Optional) Additional topics to explore this week: Bumps and Cuts, Hormones *(from the DK First Human Body Encyclopedia)*

Discussion Questions

After reading the selected pages from the encyclopedias, ask the following questions in your discussion time:

Heart

- ? What is the job of the heart?
- ? What controls our heartbeat?

Blood Vessels

? What do blood vessels do?

? What is the difference between arteries and veins?

Blood

? What does blood do?

? What are the four components of blood?

(Optional) Additional Books

- *The Heart: Our Circulatory System* by Seymour Simon
- *The Circulatory Story* by Mary K. Corcoran
- *The Amazing Circulatory System: How Does My Heart Work?* by John Burstein
- *Hear Your Heart (Let's-Read-and-Find... Science 2)* by Paul Showers and Holly Keller
- *The Magic School Bus Has a Heart* by Anne Capeci and Carolyn Bracken

Notebooking

Writing Assignments

- **Narration Page –** Have the students dictate, copy, or write one to four sentences for the heart, blood vessels and blood on SW pg. 62. They can include information that they find interesting on each topic or material that you would like them to remember. (*See the Human Body Week 1 for a sample.*)

- **(Optional) Lapbook –** Complete the Circulatory System Tab-book on pg. 44 from *Biology for the Grammar Stage Lapbooking Templates*. Have the students cut out the pages and color the cover. Then, have them tell you the purpose (or job) of the circulatory system and record it on the purpose page. After that, have the students tell you what they have learned about the heart and blood vessels. Write it for them on the respective pages. Next, have the students label the different cells on the blood page. Finally, staple the pages together and glue the tab-book into the lapbook.

Vocabulary

The following definition is a guide. The students' definitions do not need to match word for word.

- **Blood vessel –** A tube that carries blood through the body. (SW pg. 91)

Multi-week Projects and Activities

Unit Project

- **Human Body Project –** This week, have the students add the heart to the front of the body outline on SW pp. 50-51; pictures for this project are on SW pg. 111. As you add the part, do a quick oral review of the circulatory system by asking, "Do you remember what the heart does?". (**Optional** — *You could also make a life size version of this project. This week, blow up the included heart picture to wall size or have the students draw a heart on their body outline.*)
- **(Optional) Microscope Work –** Purchase a prepared slide of red blood cells to look

at under your microscope. Complete a microscope worksheet found on pg. 192 of the Appendix. If you do not own a microscope, you can view red blood cells at the following website:

- http://www.wadsworth.org/chemheme/heme/microscope/rbc.htm

Projects for this Week

- **Coloring Pages –** You can have the students color the following pages from *Biology for the Grammar Stage Coloring Pages*: Heart pg. 79, Blood Vessels pg. 80, Blood pg. 81.
- **Heart –** Have the students use a paper towel tube to listen to each others' heartbeats. Simply place the tube over a student's heart and put your ear up to the other end of the tube. You should hear the person's heart beating.
- **Blood Vessels –** Have the students write out where the pathway of the blood through the body is on the pathways of blood worksheet found in the Appendix on pg. 195. They should also draw the pathway on the image provided using red for the arteries and blue for the veins. The following is a detailed explanation of the path of blood through the body. The amount of detail your students include will depend upon their age.
    - *Oxygen poor blood enters the right atrium and flows into the right ventricle. It is then pumped out to the lungs via the pulmonary artery. The blood receives oxygen in the lungs. Then, oxygen rich blood enters the left atrium via the pulmonary veins and flows into the left ventricle. It is then pumped out to the body via the aorta and arteries. Blood is distributed to the body via the capillaries, where oxygen is removed. It is then returned to the heart via the superior and inferior vena cava and the cycle begins again.*
- **Blood –** Have the students make a model of the blood. You will need 2 cups of apple juice (*plasma*), several large marshmallows (*white blood cells*), 3 cups of red fruit loops(*red blood cells*) a handful of cinnamon red hots (*platelets*), and a large glass jar. Mix all the above ingredients together and observe what happens. (*The ingredients will float in the juice and the mixture will appear to turn red. This is just like blood in which the color comes from the red blood cells.*)

Memorization

- This week, add the following lines from *The Systems of the Human Body* poem. (SW pg. 102)

  <u>The Systems of the Human Body</u>
  The circulatory system
  Keeps blood afloat

Quiz

Weekly Quiz

- "Human Body Unit Week 6 Quiz" on SW pg. Q-30.

Quiz Answers

1. Pumps
2. Blood vessels
3. False (*Red blood cells carry oxygen around the body.*)
4. Answers will vary

Possible Schedules for Week 6

Two Days a Week Schedule	
Day 1	**Day 2**
❑ Read Boom, Boom (or Heart and Circulation) ❑ Add information about the heart to the students' Narration Page ❑ Do the Scientific Demonstration: Heartbeat ❑ Work on memorizing *The Systems of the Human Body* poem	❑ Read Blood Flow and Blood Cells (or Blood) ❑ Complete the Narration Page for this week ❑ Define blood vessel ❑ Add to the Human Body Project ❑ Take the Human Body Week 6 quiz

Five Days a Week Schedule				
Day 1	**Day 2**	**Day 3**	**Day 4**	**Day 5**
❑ Read Boom, Boom (or Heart and Circulation) ❑ Add information about the heart to the students' Narration Page ❑ Do the Heart Project	❑ Read Blood Flow ❑ Add information about the blood vessels to the students' Narration Page ❑ Do the Blood Vessels Project ❑ Add to the Human Body Project	❑ Read Blood Cells (or Blood) ❑ Add information about the blood to the students' Narration Page ❑ Do the Blood Project	❑ Do the Scientific Demonstration: Heartbeat ❑ Define blood vessel	❑ Take the Human Body Week 6 quiz ❑ Do the optional microscope work
All Week Long ❑ Work on memorizing *The Systems of the Human Body* poem				

Notes

Week 7: The Respiratory System Lesson Plans

Scientific Demonstration: Lung Capacity

Supplies Needed

- ✓ Plastic dishpan
- ✓ 2 Feet of aquarium tubing
- ✓ 1 Gallon plastic jug
- ✓ Masking tape
- ✓ Pen

Purpose

This demonstration is meant to help the students to measure how much air they can force out of their lungs.

Instructions and Explanation

The instructions and explanation for this scientific demonstration are found on pp. 186-187 of *Janice VanCleave's Biology for Every Kid*. Have the students complete the Lab Report on SW pg. 65.

Take it Further

Have the students have a breathing race. You will need several cotton balls and straws for this activity. Mark a start and finish line at either end of a long table. Have the students sit at the start end of a long table. Then, have each of them place a cotton ball on the start line in front of them. When you say go, have the students try to blow their cotton ball to the finish line. The first one to get there wins the race.

Science-Oriented Books

Reading Assignments

- *DK First Human Body Encyclopedia pp. 62-63 (Air and Oxygen), pp. 60-61 (Air Bags), pp. 64-65 (Making Sounds)*
- *Kingfisher Science Encyclopedia pp. 124-125 (Lungs and Breathing)*

(Optional) Additional topic to explore this week: Ah-choo! *(from the DK First Human Body Encyclopedia)*

Discussion Questions

After reading the selected pages from the encyclopedias, ask the following questions in your discussion time:

Lungs

- ? What is the job of the lungs?
- ? What do the lungs look like?

Alveoli

- ? What do the alveoli do?

? Where can the alveoli be found?

Breathing

? What is inhalation?

? What is exhalation?

(Optional) Additional Books

- *The Respiratory System: Why Do I Feel Out of Breath?* by Sue Barraclough
- *How Do Your Lungs Work? (Rookie Read-About Health)* by Don L. Curry
- *The Remarkable Respiratory System: How Do My Lungs Work?* by John Burstein
- *Breathe In, Breathe Out: Learning About Your Lungs (Amazing Body)* by Pamela Hill Nettleton

Notebooking

Writing Assignments

- **Narration Page** – Have the students dictate, copy, or write one to four sentences for the lungs, alveoli, and breathing on SW pg. 64. They can include information that they find interesting on each topic or material that you would like them to remember. (*See the Human Body Week 1 for a sample.*)

- **(Optional) Lapbook** – Complete the Respiratory System Tab-book on pg. 46 from *Biology for the Grammar Stage Lapbooking Templates*. Have the students cut out the pages and color the cover. Then, have them tell you the purpose (or job) of the respiratory system and record it on the purpose page. After that, have the students tell you what they have learned about the lungs and alveoli. Write it for them on the respective pages. Finally, staple the pages together and glue the tab-book into the lapbook.

Vocabulary

The following definition is a guide. The students' definitions do not need to match word for word.

- **Alveoli** – Tiny air bags found in your lungs. (SW pg. 90)

Multi-week Projects and Activities

Unit Project

- **Human Body Project** – This week, have the students add the lungs to the front of the body outline on SW pp. 50-51; pictures for this project are on SW pg. 111. As you add the part, do a quick oral review of the respiratory system by asking, "Do you remember what the lungs does?". (**Optional** — *You could also make a life size version of this project. This week, blow up the included lungs picture to wall size or have the students draw the lungs on their body outline.*)
- **(Optional) Microscope Work** – Purchase a prepared slide of lung cells to look at under your microscope. Complete a microscope worksheet found on pg. 192 of the Appendix.

If you do not own a microscope, you can view lung cells at the following website:
- http://sydney.edu.au/science/biology/learning/lung_disorders/HealthyLT.shtml

Projects for this Week

- **Coloring Pages** – You can have the students color the following pages from *Biology for the Grammar Stage Coloring Pages*: Lungs pg. 82, Alveoli pg. 83, Breathing pg. 84.
- **Lungs** – Have the students make their own model of the lungs using a plastic bottle, straw, and balloons. You can find directions for this project at the following website:
  - https://www.questacon.edu.au/outreach/programs/science-circus/videos/model-of-lung
- **Alveoli** – Have the students demonstrate that there is water vapor in their breath. You will need a mirror for this activity. Have the students hold the mirror close to their mouth and then breathe out on it. What happens to the mirror? (*It should fog up.*) This is due to the water vapor found in the air we exhale.
- **Breathing** – Have the students complete the Inhalation vs. Exhalation worksheet on pg. 196 of the Appendix. They should label each process and what happens during them. Here are the answers for your reference.

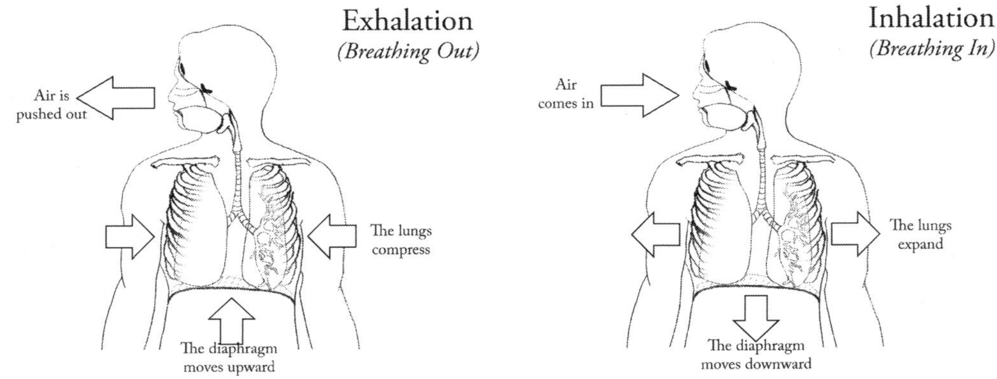

Memorization

- This week, add the following lines from *The Systems of the Human Body* poem. (SW pg. 102)

  The Systems of the Human Body

  The respiratory system
  Breathes in and out

Quiz

Weekly Quiz

- "Human Body Unit Week 7 Quiz" on SW pg. Q-31.

Quiz Answers

1. True
2. Oxygen, Carbon dioxide
3. False (*Alveoli are tiny air bags found in your lungs.*)
4. Answers will vary

Possible Schedules for Week 7

Two Days a Week Schedule	
Day 1	**Day 2**
❑ Read Air and Oxygen (or Lungs and Breathing ~ 1st half) ❑ Add information about the lungs to the students' Narration Page ❑ Do the Scientific Demonstration: Lung Capacity ❑ Work on memorizing *The Systems of the Human Body* poem	❑ Read Air Bags and Making Sounds (or Lungs and Breathing ~ 2nd half) ❑ Complete the Narration Page for this week ❑ Define alveoli ❑ Add to the Human Body Project ❑ Take the Human Body Week 7 quiz

Five Days a Week Schedule				
Day 1	**Day 2**	**Day 3**	**Day 4**	**Day 5**
❑ Read Air and Oxygen (or Lungs and Breathing ~ 1st half) ❑ Add information about the lungs to the students' Narration Page ❑ Do the Lungs Project	❑ Read Air Bags ❑ Add information about the alveoli to the students' Narration Page ❑ Do the Blood Vessels Project ❑ Add to the Alveoli Project	❑ Do the Scientific Demonstration: Lung Capacity ❑ Define alveoli	❑ Read Making Sounds (or Lungs and Breathing ~ 2nd half) ❑ Add information about breathing to the students' Narration Page ❑ Do the Breathing Project	❑ Take the Human Body Week 7 quiz ❑ Do the optional microscope work
All Week Long ❑ Work on memorizing *The Systems of the Human Body* poem				

Notes

Week 8: The Digestive System Lesson Plans

Scientific Demonstration: Folds

Supplies Needed

- ✓ Paper towels
- ✓ Slender glass jar
- ✓ Masking tape
- ✓ Marking pen

Purpose

This demonstration is meant to help the students to see how the shape of the intestines increases absorbency.

Instructions and Explanation

The instructions and explanation for this scientific demonstration are found on pp. 198-199 of *Janice VanCleave's Biology for Every Kid*. Have the students complete the Lab Report on SW pg. 67.

Take it Further

Add a third trial using 5 paper towels. (*The students should see that the increased number of paper towels were able to absorb more water.*)

Science-Oriented Books

Reading Assignments

- *DK First Human Body Encyclopedia pp. 82-83 (Digestive System), pp. 84-85 (Chew it Over), pp. 88-89 (Inside Intestines)*
- *Kingfisher Science Encyclopedia pp. 128-129 (Digestion), pg. 127 (Teeth)*

(Optional) Additional topic to explore this week: From mouth to stomach *(from the DK First Human Body Encyclopedia)*

Discussion Questions

After reading the selected pages from the encyclopedias, ask the following questions in your discussion time:

Digestive System

- ? What is the purpose of the digestive system?
- ? What is digestion?

Teeth

- ? What do teeth do?
- ? How many teeth do adults have? Children?

Intestines

- ? What happens in the intestines?
- ? How are the small intestines different from the large intestines?

(Optional) Additional Books

- *What Happens to a Hamburger? (Let's-Read-and-Find... Science 2)* by Paul Showers
- *Where Does Your Food Go? (Rookie Read-About Health)* by Wiley Blevins
- *The Dynamic Digestive System: How Does My Stomach Work?* by John Burstein
- *Guts: Our Digestive System* by Seymour Simon

Notebooking

Writing Assignments

- **Narration Page** – Have the students dictate, copy, or write one to four sentences for the digestive system, teeth and intestines on SW pg. 66. They can include information that they find interesting on each topic or material that you would like them to remember. (*See the Human Body Week 1 for a sample.*)

- **(Optional) Lapbook** – Begin the Digestive and Urinary Systems Accordion Fold-book on pg. 47 from *Biology for the Grammar Stage Lapbooking Templates*. Have the students cut out the page and color the pictures. Then, have them tell you the purpose (or job) of the digestive system and record it on the correct block. After that, have the students tell you what they have learned about the teeth and intestines. Write it for them on the respective blocks. The students will finish the fold-book next week.

Vocabulary

The following definition is a guide. The students' definitions do not need to match word for word.

- **Digestion** – The process by which your food is broken down. (SW pg. 92)

Multi-week Projects and Activities

Unit Project

- **Human Body Project** – This week, have the students add the digestive system to the front of the body outline on SW pp. 50-51; pictures for this project are on SW pg. 111. As you add the part, do a quick oral review of the digestive system by asking, "How does food move through the digestive system?". (**Optional** — *You could also make a life size version of this project. This week, blow up the included digestive system picture to wall size or have the students draw an outline of the stomach and intestines on their body outline.*)
- **(Optional) Microscope Work** – Purchase a prepared slide of salivary gland cells to look at under your microscope. Complete a microscope worksheet found on pg. 192 of the Appendix. If you do not own a microscope, you can view salivary gland cells at the following website:
  - http://www.histol.chuvashia.com/atlas-en/digestive-04-en.htm

Projects for this Week

- **Coloring Pages** – You can have the students color the following pages from *Biology for the Grammar Stage Coloring Pages*: Digestive System pg. 85, Teeth pg. 86, Intestines pg. 87.

- ✂ **Digestive System –** Have the students make a model of the stomach. You will need a large Ziploc bag, bread and coke. Have the students open the bag and add several pieces of bread. Have them mush up the bread with their hands, simulating what happens when they chew up the bread. Then, have them add 1 cup of coke to simulate stomach acid. Continue to squeeze and shake the bag around to see what happens to the bread. (*The bread should break down into a pulp, just like what happens to our food in the stomach.*)
- ✂ **Teeth –** Share with your students about dental health. The following website from the American Dental Association has presentations and activities to help you with this:
  - http://www.ada.org/387.aspx
- ✂ **Intestines –** Have the students create a Venn diagram explaining the similarities and differences between the small and large intestines. You can use the worksheet provided on pg. __ of the Appendix in this guide. Simply have the students color either the small or large intestines in the two pictures and then write the similarities where the two circles overlap and differences in the individual circles. Here are a few to get you started:

Small Intestines	Both	Large Intestines
Breaks down food; Absorbs nutrients; Is very long; Has villi	Are lined with mucus; Are part of the digestive tract.	Produces stool (or feces); Absorbs water; Eliminates waste.

Memorization

This week, add the following lines from *The Systems of the Human Body* poem. (SW pg. 102)

<u>**The Systems of the Human Body**</u>
The digestive system
Breaks down the trout

Quiz

Weekly Quiz

- "Human Body Unit Week 8 Quiz" on SW pg. Q-32.

Quiz Answers

1. Broken down
2. Your teeth
3. True
4. Answers will vary

Possible Schedules for Week 8

Two Days a Week Schedule	
Day 1	**Day 2**
❑ Read Inside Intestines (or Digestion) ❑ Add information about the intestines to the students' Narration Page ❑ Do the Scientific Demonstration: Folds ❑ Work on memorizing *The Systems of the Human Body* poem	❑ Read Digestive System or Chew it Over (or Teeth) ❑ Complete the Narration Page for this week ❑ Define digestion ❑ Add to the Human Body Project ❑ Take the Human Body Week 8 quiz

Five Days a Week Schedule				
Day 1	**Day 2**	**Day 3**	**Day 4**	**Day 5**
❑ Read Digestive System (or Digestion) ❑ Add information about the digestive system to the students' Narration Page ❑ Do the Digestive System Project	❑ Read Chew it Over (or Teeth) ❑ Add information about the teeth to the students' Narration Page ❑ Do the Teeth Project	❑ Read Inside Intestines ❑ Add information about the intestines to the students' Narration Page ❑ Do the Intestines Project	❑ Do the Scientific Demonstration: Folds ❑ Define digestion ❑ Add to the Human Body Project	❑ Take the Human Body Week 8 quiz ❑ Do the optional microscope work
All Week Long ❑ Work on memorizing *The Systems of the Human Body* poem				

Notes

Week 9: The Urinary System (plus Genes) Lesson Plans

Scientific Demonstration: Picture Family Tree

Supplies Needed

- ✓ Family pictures

Purpose

This demonstration is meant to help the students to see the similarities between people that are genetically related.

Instructions

Gather together pictures of the students' families up to their grandparents. Start by placing the individual students at the bottom of their lab sheet on SW pg. 69. Next, place any siblings they have to the right and left. Then, place their parents above them and add any aunts and uncles to the right of them. Place any cousins the students may have under the aunts and uncles. Finally, place their grandparents above the students' parents. Once their picture family tree, take some time to discuss the genetic similarities in the students' families (e.g. discuss how their family members look alike).

Take it Further

Expand the project to include more of the students' family.

Science-Oriented Books

Reading Assignments

(Note — *If you wish to present reproduction to your students this week, I recommend that you read the suggested sections under the additional topics.*)

- *DK First Human Body Encyclopedia pp. 90-91 (Waterworks), pp. 92-93 (Stretchy Bladder), pp. 6-7 (What makes you you?)*
- *Kingfisher Science Encyclopedia pp. 131(Waste Disposal), pg. 135 (Genes and Chromosomes)*

(Optional) Additional topics to explore this week: Making a baby, Growing in the womb *(from the DK First Human Body Encyclopedia)*

Discussion Questions

After reading the selected pages from the encyclopedias, ask the following questions in your discussion time:

Urinary System

- ? What is the purpose of the urinary system?
- ? What do the kidneys do?

Bladder

- ? What does the bladder do?
- ? How far can the bladder stretch?

Genes and DNA

- ? What do the genes do?

? What is DNA?

(Optional) Additional Books

- *The Digestive and Excretory Systems (The Human Body Library)* by Susan Dudley Gold
- *Learning about the Digestive and Excretory Systems (Learning about the Human Body Systems)* by Susan Dudley Gold
- *My Messy Body (Body Works)* by Liza Fromer, Francine and Joe Weissmann
- *Have a Nice DNA (Enjoy Your Cells, 3)* by Fran Balkwill and Mic Rolph

Notebooking

Writing Assignments

- **Narration Page** – Have the students dictate, copy, or write one to four sentences for the urinary system, bladder, and genes on SW pg. 68. They can include information that they find interesting on each topic or material that you would like them to remember. (*See the Human Body Week 1 for a sample.*)

- **(Optional) Lapbook** – Complete the Digestive and Urinary Systems Accordion Fold-book on pg. 47 from *Biology for the Grammar Stage Lapbooking Templates*. Have the students cut out the page and color the pictures. Then, have them tell you the purpose (or job) of the urinary system and record it on the correct block. After that, have the students tell you what they have learned about the kidneys. Write it for them on the respective block. Finally, fold the book like an accordion and glue the back into the lapbook.

Vocabulary

The following definition is a guide. The students' definitions do not need to match word for word.

- **Kidney** – The organ in the body responsible for removing waste from itself and regulating the body's fluid levels. (SW pg. 94)

Multi-week Projects and Activities

Unit Project

- **Human Body Project** – This is the last week for this project. Have the students add the urinary system to the front of the body outline on SW pp. 50-51; pictures for this project are on SW pg. 111. As you add the part, do a quick oral review of the urinary system by asking, "What are this part and what does it do?". (**Optional** — *You could also make a life size version of this project. This week, blow up the included urinary system picture to wall size or have the students draw an outline of the kidneys and bladder on their body outline.*)

Projects for this Week

- **Coloring Pages** – You can have the students color the following pages from *Biology for the Grammar Stage Coloring Pages*: Urinary System pg. 88, DNA pg. 89.
- **Urinary System** – Watch a video about the body this week. The following to movies

are good options: *(Please preview each video before allowing the students to watch it to make sure it is appropriate for your group.)*

- *The Magic School Bus: Human Body*
- *The Magic School Bus: Inside Ralphie*

✂ **Stretchy Bladder** – You will need a balloon, funnel and water for this activity. Have the students use the funnel to fill the balloon with water one cup at a time. Observe how the balloon stretches to accommodate the water, but at some point it reaches full capacity. Then have the students pour the water out and see if the balloon has changed. (*The students should see that the balloon can contain several cups of water, but when the water is poured out it returns to its original shape. This is just like the bladder in the human body. It stretches to store the urine produced by the body and returns to its original shape once it is emptied.*)

✂ **Genes and DNA** – Have the students build their own DNA ladders. You will need four different colors of blocks (*at least six of each*). Have the students build a Lego tower that is fifteen rows high with the four different colors to see how many combos they can get. Explain to the students that certain colors can only pair with other colors and that each row can only have two blocks, just like DNA. They should be able to come up with many different combinations.

Memorization

This week, add the following lines from *The Systems of the Human Body* poem. (SW pg. 102)

<u>The Systems of the Human Body</u>
The urinary system
Could fill a moat

Quiz

Weekly Quiz

- "Human Body Unit Week 9 Quiz" on SW pg. Q-33.

Quiz Answers

1. False (*The bladder can stretch.*)
2. Waste
3. True
4. Answers will vary

Notes

Possible Schedules for Week 9

Two Days a Week Schedule	
Day 1	**Day 2**
❑ Read What makes you you? (or Genes and Chromosomes) ❑ Add information about the genes and DNA to the students' Narration Page ❑ Do the Scientific Demonstration: Picture Family Tree ❑ Work on memorizing *The Systems of the Human Body* poem	❑ Read Waterworks and Stretchy Bladder (or Waste Disposal) ❑ Complete the Narration Page for this week ❑ Define kidney ❑ Complete the Human Body Project ❑ Take the Human Body Week 9 quiz

Five Days a Week Schedule				
Day 1	**Day 2**	**Day 3**	**Day 4**	**Day 5**
❑ Read Waterworks (or Waste Disposal) ❑ Add information about the urinary system to the students' Narration Page ❑ Do the Urinary System Project ❑ Define kidney	❑ Read Stretchy Bladder ❑ Add information about the bladder to the students' Narration Page ❑ Do the Bladder Project	❑ Read What makes you you? (or Genes and Chromosomes) ❑ Add information about the genes and DNA to the students' Narration Page ❑ Do the Genes and DNA Project	❑ Do the Scientific Demonstration: Picture Family Tree	❑ Take the Human Body Week 9 quiz ❑ Complete the Human Body Project
All Week Long ❑ Work on memorizing *The Systems of the Human Body* poem				

Notes

Week 10: The Immune System Lesson Plans

Scientific Demonstration: Bacterial Growth

Supplies Needed

- ✓ Milk
- ✓ Measuring cup
- ✓ 2 Pint jars

Purpose

This demonstration is meant to help the students to see how temperature effects the growth of bacteria.

Instructions and Explanation

The instructions and explanation for this scientific demonstration are found on pp. 84-87 of *Janice VanCleave's Biology for Every Kid*. Have the students complete the Lab Report on SW pg. 71.

Take it Further

Do the demonstrations entitled "Coconut Cultures" found on pp. 88-89 of *Janice VanCleave's Biology for Every Kid* with the students.

Science-Oriented Books

Reading Assignments

- *DK First Human Body Encyclopedia pp. 74-75 (Germs), pg. 76-77 (Body Defenses), pp. 80-81 (Allergies)*
- *Kingfisher Science Encyclopedia pg. 136 (Bacteria and Viruses), pg. 137 (The Immune System), pg. 138 (Diseases)*

(Optional) Additional topic to explore this week: Fighting Germs*(from the DK First Human Body Encyclopedia)*

Discussion Questions

After reading the selected pages from the encyclopedias, ask the following questions in your discussion time:

Germs

- ? What are germs?
- ? What do germs cause the body to do?

Body Defenses

- ? What system is responsible for defending the body against disease?
- ? What are white blood cells?

Allergies

- ? What are allergies?
- ? What causes allergies

(Optional) Additional Books

- *The Immune System Your Magic Doctor: A Guide to the Immune System for the Curious of All Ages* by Helen Garvy and Dan Bessie
- *Body Warriors: The Immune System* by Lisa Trumbauer
- *Our Immune System (Our Bodies (Discovery Library))* by Susan Thames
- *Germs* by Ross Collins

Notebooking

Writing Assignments

- **Narration Page –** Have the students dictate, copy, or write one to four sentences for the germs, body defenses, and allergies on SW pg. 70. They can include information that they find interesting on each topic or material that you would like them to remember. (*See the Human Body Week 1 for a sample.*)
- **(Optional) Lapbook –** Complete the Immune System Tab-book on pg. 48 from *Biology for the Grammar Stage Lapbooking Templates*. Have the students cut out the pages and color the cover. Then, have them tell you the purpose (or job) of the immune system and record it on the purpose page. After that, have the students tell you what they have learned about germs and the body's defenses. Write it for them on the respective pages. Finally, staple the pages together and glue the tab-book into the lapbook.

Vocabulary

The following definition is a guide. The students' definitions do not need to match word for word.

- **Bacteria –** A group of microscopic organisms that can cause diseases. (SW pg. 90)

Multi-week Projects and Activities

Unit Project

- There are no unit projects to complete this week.

Projects for this Week

- **Coloring Pages –** You can have the students color the following pages from *Biology for the Grammar Stage Coloring Pages*: Germs pg. 90, White Blood Cell pg. 91.
- **Germs –** Have the students determine which room has the most germs. You will need sterile cotton swaps, petri dishes, and agar. Use the cotton swabs to test different areas in several rooms in the house. See the following website for directions for this process:
  - http://www.ehow.com/how_6381785_test-bacteria-kitchen-counters.html
- **Body Defenses –** Have the students make a well vs. sick poster. You will need a several magazines, glue, and poster board. Have the students cut out pictures of healthy foods and activities for the body and things that are unhealthy for the body. Have them divide the poster into two sections, label one section "well" and the other "sick". Then, have the

students glue the healthy pictures, such as vegetables, fruit, or exercise, on the "well" side of the poster. Have them glue the sick pictures, such as cigarettes and fatty foods, on the "sick" side of the poster.

- ✂ **Allergies –** Awareness of food allergies in the United States is on the rise. Now days, all food packaging must have allergy warnings. Have the students go through their pantry and find the foods can cause allergies. Then, have them sort the box or cans into allergy groups (e.g. not safe for people with peanut allergies, not safe for people with wheat allergies, and so on.) If you know someone with a food allergy, be sure to share more about their situation with your students.

Memorization

- Finish memorizing the *The Systems of the Human Body* poem. (SW pg. 102)

<u>The Systems of the Human Body</u>

The skeletal system
Holds me upright

The muscular system
Moves me all night

The nervous system
Sends cells a note

The circulatory system
Keeps blood afloat

The respiratory system
Breathes in and out

The digestive system
Breaks down the trout

The urinary system
Could fill a moat

The immune system
Fixes strep throat

Quiz

Weekly Quiz

- "Human Body Unit Week 10 Quiz" on SW pg. Q-34.

Quiz Answers

1. True
2. Microscopic
3. Immune
4. Answers will vary

Notes

Possible Schedules for Week 10

Two Days a Week Schedule	
Day 1	**Day 2**
❑ Read Germs (or Bacteria and Viruses) ❑ Add information about germs to the students' Narration Page ❑ Do the Scientific Demonstration: Bacterial Growth ❑ Work on memorizing *The Systems of the Human Body* poem	❑ Read Body Defenses and Allergies (or The Immune System and Diseases) ❑ Complete the Narration Page for this week ❑ Define bacteria ❑ Finish the Bacterial Growth Demonstration ❑ Take the Human Body Week 10 quiz

Five Days a Week Schedule				
Day 1	**Day 2**	**Day 3**	**Day 4**	**Day 5**
❑ Begin the Scientific Demonstration: Bacterial Growth ❑ Define bacteria	❑ Read Germs (or Bacteria and Viruses) ❑ Add information about germs to the students' Narration Page ❑ Do the Germs Project	❑ Read Body Defenses (or The Immune System) ❑ Add information about the body defenses to the students' Narration Page ❑ Do the Body Defenses Project	❑ Read Allergies (or Diseases) ❑ Add information about allergies to the students' Narration Page ❑ Do the Allergies Project	❑ Take the Human Body Week 10 quiz ❑ Finish the Bacterial Growth Demonstration
All Week Long ❑ Work on memorizing *The Systems of the Human Body* poem				

Biology for the Grammar Stage

Plants Unit

Plants Unit Overview
(6 weeks)

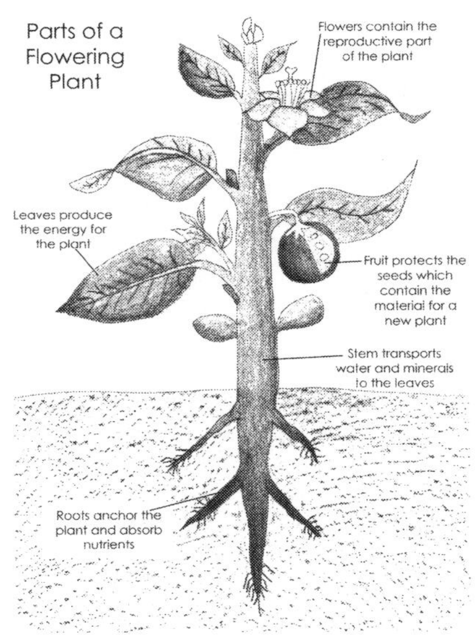
Parts of a Flowering Plant
Flowers contain the reproductive part of the plant
Leaves produce the energy for the plant
Fruit protects the seeds which contain the material for a new plant
Stem transports water and minerals to the leaves
Roots anchor the plant and absorb nutrients

Books Scheduled

Encyclopedias

- *Basher Science: Biology - Life as we know it!*

  OR

- *Usborne Science Encyclopedia*

Scientific Demonstration Book

- *Janice VanCleave's Biology for Every Kid*

Sequence for Study

- **Week 1:** Leaves
- **Week 2:** Flowers
- **Week 3:** Fruits and Seeds
- **Week 4:** Nuts, Cones, and Spores
- **Week 5:** Stems
- **Week 6:** Roots

Plant Poems to Memorize

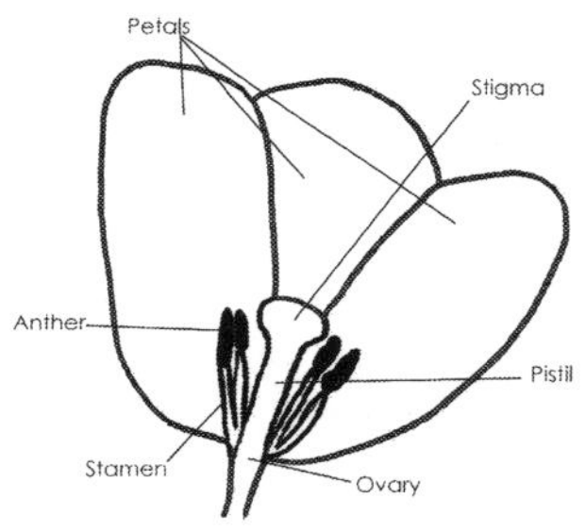
Petals
Stigma
Anther
Pistil
Stamen
Ovary

Parts of a Flower

The bud becomes a flower
It's happening this very hour
The flower has petals so bright
It attracts the insect in flight
The stamen provides the pollen it needs
To join with the pistil and make a seed

Parts of a Plant

The plant stem holds it up high
The leaves reach way up to the sky
It has roots that go into the ground
Gathering nutrients and keeping balance sound

Supplies Needed for the Unit

Week	Supplies needed
1	Alcohol, Green leaf, Coffee filter, Pencil, Baby food jar, Ruler

Week	Supplies needed
2	Measuring cup, 2 Glasses, 1 White carnation with long stem, Red and blue food coloring
3	10 or 12 Dry pinto beans, Jar, Paper towels
4	Pine cone (tightly closed), Magnifying glass
5	1 Glass, A piece of wilted celery, Blue food coloring
6	Paper towels, 4 Pinto beans, Masking tape, Drinking glass, Marking pen

Unit Vocabulary

1. **Leaf** – The part of the plant that makes the food for the plant.
2. **Bud** – A swelling on a plant stem containing tiny flower parts ready to burst into a bloom.
3. **Flower** – The reproductive parts of a plant.
4. **Seed** – The part of the plant that contains the beginnings of a new plant.
5. **Cone** – A type of dry fruit produced by a conifer.
6. **Stem** – The part of the plant that holds it upright and supports the leaves and flowers.
7. **Roots** – The part of the plant that anchors the plant firmly to the ground and absorbs water and nutrients.

Week 1: Leaves Lesson Plans

Scientific Demonstration: Leaf Colors

Supplies Needed

- ✓ Alcohol
- ✓ Green leaf
- ✓ Coffee filter
- ✓ Pencil
- ✓ Baby food jar
- ✓ Ruler

Purpose

This demonstration is meant to help the students to see the different colors in a leaf.

Instructions and Explanation

The instructions and explanation for this scientific demonstration are found on pp. 38-39 of *Janice VanCleave's Biology for Every Kid*. Have the students complete the Lab Report on SW pg. 77.

Take it Further

Repeat the demonstration with different colored leaves to see if you get a different result. (*The students should see different colors. For example, if the leaf is orange, they will see red and yellow.*)

Science-Oriented Books

Reading Assignments

- *Basher Biology pg. 114 (Leaves), pg. 112 (Chlorophyll)*
- *Usborne Science Encyclopedia pp. 258-259 (Leaves), pp. 264 (Plant Food)*

(Optional) Additional topic to explore this week: Leaf Structure (USE pp. 260-261)

Discussion Questions

After reading the selected pages from the encyclopedias, ask the following questions in your discussion time:

Leaves

- ? What does the leaf do for a plant?
- ? Are all leaves the same color, size, and shape?

Photosynthesis

- ? What does chlorophyll do?
- ? What is photosynthesis?

(Optional) Additional Books

- *Why Do Leaves Change Color? (Let's-Read-and-Find... Science, Stage 2)* by Betsy Maestro
- *Leaves (Designs for Coloring)* by Ruth Heller

- *Leaf Jumpers* by Carole Gerber
- *Leaves* by David Ezra Stein
- *Photosynthesis: Changing Sunlight Into Food (Nature's Changes)* by Bobbie Kalman

Notebooking

Writing Assignments

- **Narration Page** – Have the students dictate, copy, or write one to four sentences on what they have learned about leaves and photosynthesis on SW pg. 76. For example, this week, the student could dictate, copy, or write the following for leaves:

  They are different from each other.
  They change color to brown when they die.
  The leaves make the plant's food.

- **(Optional) Lapbook** – Throughout this unit, the students can complete a Parts of a Plant Tab-book. For this week, have the students cut out and color the cover and leaves page on pg. 51 from *Biology for the Grammar Stage Lapbooking Templates*. Ask the students what they have learned about leaves this week and then add their narration to that page of the tab-book. Have them color the pictures on the two sheets and save them until they assemble the booklet in the last week of the unit.

Vocabulary

The following definition is a guide. The students' definitions do not need to match word for word.

- **Leaf** – The part of the plant that makes the food for the plant. (SW pg. 94)

Multi-week Projects and Activities

Unit Project

- **Plant Growth Project** – During this unit, the students will record the growth of a bean plant. This week, have the students begin this project by planting their seeds. They will need dirt, a small pot, water, and a pinto bean seed. Have them fill the pot with dirt and gently press the bean seed just under the surface of the dirt. Have them water the pot well before placing it on a windowsill that receives direct sun light. Over the week, have them check their pots and water the plant when the soil is dry. On Friday, have them measure and record how much it has grown on the Plant Growth Record Chart on SW pg. 75.
- **(Optional) Nature Walk Sheets** – Each week, take a nature walk to look for flowers and unique leaves. If possible, have the students collect the leaves to take them home and press; if not, take a picture of the samples. Once you are back at home, have the students identify the flowers and leaves they found using a field guide book from the library or the Internet. Have them record their findings on a Nature Walk Sheet found in the Appendix of this guide on pg. 198.

Projects for this Week

- ✂ **Coloring Pages –** You can have the students color the following pages from *Biology for the Grammar Stage Coloring Pages*: Leaves pg. 92, Photosynthesis pg. 93.
- ✂ **Leaves –** Have the students make a leaf rubbing booklet. Go on a nature walk and collect several different kinds of leaves—try to include pine needles in the collection. Once at home, have the students use the samples to make a booklet of leaf rubbings. Have them begin this process by identifying the leaves they have collected. Then, have them place each leaf under a piece of paper and rub on the top of the same paper with a crayon until the shape of the leaf appears. Have them label the page with the type of leaf and set it aside. Once they have created a page for each of the leaves, have them bind the book together and create a cover.
- ✂ **Photosynthesis –** Have the students test to see if light is really necessary for photosynthesis. They will neeed a live plant and a dark room, like a closet, for this activity. Have the students place the plant in the dark room where it will not receive any light for three days. Have them check the plant every day and observe what happens. After three days, have them place the plant back in the full sun and observe what happens over the next few days. Be sure to have the students water the plant as needed througout the week.

Memorization

This week, begin working on memorizing the *Parts of a Flower* poem. (SW pg. 103)

<u>Parts of a Flower</u>

The bud becomes a flower
It's happening this very hour
The flower has petals so bright
It attracts the insect in flight
The stamen provides the pollen it needs
To join with the pistil and make a seed

Quiz

Weekly Quiz

- "Plants Unit Week 1 Quiz" on SW pg. Q-35.

Quiz Answers

1. Leaf
2. Photosynthesis
3. True
4. Answers will vary

Possible Schedules for Week 1

Two Days a Week Schedule	
❑ Read about Leaves ❑ Add information on leaves to the Narration Page ❑ Do the Scientific Demonstration: Leaf Color ❑ Begin the Plant Growth Project ❑ Define leaf	❑ Read about Chlorophyll (or Plant Food) ❑ Add information on photosynthesis to the weekly Narration Page ❑ Measure and record the growth of your plant for the Plant Growth Project ❑ Work on memorizing the *Parts of a Flower* poem ❑ Take the Plants Week 1 quiz

Five Days a Week Schedule				
❑ Begin the Plant Growth Project ❑ Define leaf	❑ Read about Leaves ❑ Add information on leaves to the Narration Page ❑ Do the Leaves Project	❑ Do the Scientific Demonstration: Leaf Color	❑ Read about Chlorophyll (or Plant Food) ❑ Add information on photosynthesis to the Narration Page ❑ Do the Photosynthesis Project	❑ Take the Plants Week 1 quiz ❑ Measure and record the growth of your plant for the Plant Growth Project
All Week Long ❑ Work on memorizing the *Parts of a Flower* poem				

Notes

Week 2: Flowers Lesson Plans

Scientific Demonstration: Water Flow

Supplies Needed

- ✓ Measuring cup
- ✓ 2 Glasses
- ✓ 1 White carnation with a long stem
- ✓ Red and blue food coloring

Purpose

This demonstration is meant to help the students to see how water is transported through plant stems.

Instructions and Explanation

The instructions and explanation for this scientific demonstration are found on pp. 18-19 of *Janice VanCleave's Biology for Every Kid*. Have the students complete the Lab Report on SW pg. 79.

Take it Further

Repeat the demonstration with different colors of food coloring or with different kinds of flowers, such as a daisy, to see if you get a different result.

Science-Oriented Books

Reading Assignments

- *Basher Biology pg. 34 (Flowering Plants), pg. 118 (Flower), pg. 120 (Pollen)*
- *Usborne Science Encyclopedia pp. 270-271 (Flowering Plants, part 1)*

(Optional) Additional topic to explore this week: Pollination (USE pp. 272-273)

Discussion Questions

After reading the selected pages from the encyclopedias, ask the following questions in your discussion time:

Flowering Plants

- ? What is common to all flowering plants?
- ? What types of plants are flowering plants?

Flowers

- ? Why do flowers have bright colors?
- ? What can flowers produce?

Pollen

- ? What is pollen?
- ? Where is the pollen produced in the flower?

(Optional) Additional Books

- *The Reason for a Flower (World of Nature)* by Ruth Heller

- *A Weed Is a Flower* by Aliki
- *Flower (Life Cycle of A…)* by Molly Aloian

Notebooking

Writing Assignments

- ☐ **Narration Page –** Have the students dictate, copy, or write one to four sentences on what they have learned for flowering plants, flowers, and pollen on SW pg. 78. They can include information that they find interesting on each topic or material that you would like them to remember. (*See Plants Week 1 for a sample.*)
- ☐ **(Optional) Lapbook –** Have the students work on their Parts of a Plant Tab-book. For this week, have the students cut out and color the cover and flowers page on pg. 52 from *Biology for the Grammar Stage Lapbooking Templates*. Ask the students what they have learned about leaves this week and then add their narration to that page of the tab-book. Have them color the pictures on the sheet and save it until they assemble the booklet in the last week of the unit.
- ☐ **(Optional) Lapbook –** Have the students complete the Pollen Mini-book on pg. 54 from *Biology for the Grammar Stage Lapbooking Templates*. Have them cut out and color the mini-book. Ask them what they have learned about pollen. Write their narration sentences on the inside of the book. Finally, glue the mini-book into the lapbook.
- ☐ **(Optional) Lapbook –** Have the students complete the Parts of a Flower Mini Tab-book on pg. 55 from *Biology for the Grammar Stage Lapbooking Templates*. Have them cut out and color the pages of the mini tab-book. Then, have them label the bud page with bud and stem, and the flower page with pistil, stamen, and petals. Finally, have the students staple the pages together and glue the mini tab-book into the lapbooks.
- ☐ **(Optional) Lapbook –** Have the students add the Parts of a Flower Poem on pg. 54 from *Biology for the Grammar Stage Lapbooking Templates* to their lapbook. Have them cut out and color the poem sheet. Once they are finished, have the students glue the poem into the lapbook.

Vocabulary

The following definitions are a guide. The students' definitions do not need to match word for word.

- **Bud –** A swelling on a plant stem containing tiny flower parts ready to burst into a bloom. (SW pg. 91)
- **Flower –** The reproductive parts of a plant. (SW pg. 93)

Multi-week Projects and Activities

Unit Project

- ✂ **Plant Growth Project –** During this unit, the students will record the growth of a bean plant. This week, have them water the plant as necessary. On Friday, have them measure and record how much it has grown on the Plant Growth Record Chart on SW pg. 75.

- ✂ **(Optional) Nature Walk Sheets –** Each week, take a nature walk to look for flowers and unique leaves. If possible, have the students collect the leaves to take them home and press; if not, take a picture of the samples. Once you are back at home, have the students identify the flowers and leaves they found using a field guide book from the library or the Internet. Have them record their findings on a Nature Walk Sheet found in the Appendix of this guide on pg. 198.

Projects for this Week

- ✂ **Coloring Pages –** You can have the students color the following pages from *Biology for the Grammar Stage Coloring Pages*: Flowering Plants pg. 94, Flowers pg. 95, Pollen pg. 96.
- ✂ **Flowering Plants –** Plant a flower box with different types of flowers with the students. As you plant the flowers, talk about the similarities and differences between the plants. Also take some time to point out the various parts you have studied so far.
- ✂ **Flowers –** Dissect a flower with the students. Purchase a lily or other flower with clearly visible parts. As you dissect the flower, be sure to point out the various parts to the students. For a more detailed explanation of this project, visit the following website:
  - https://elementalscience.com/blogs/science-activities/94044099-how-to-dissect-a-flower
- ✂ **Pollen –** Have the students learn about pollination with cheetos. You can find the directions for this project at the following website:
  - http://littlekinderwarriors.com/2011/04/pollination-science-lesson.html

Memorization

- Work on memorizing the *Parts of a Flower* poem. (SW pg. 103)

Parts of a Flower

The bud becomes a flower
It's happening this very hour
The flower has petals so bright
It attracts the insect in flight
The stamen provides the pollen it needs
To join with the pistil and make a seed

Quiz

Weekly Quiz

- "Plants Unit Week 2 Quiz" on SW pg. Q-36.

Quiz Answers

1. True
2. All
3. False (*Flowers come in many different shapes and sizes.*)
4. Answers will vary

Possible Schedules for Week 2

Two Days a Week Schedule	
❑ Read about Flowering Plants (or Flowering Plants, 1st page) ❑ Add information on flowering plants to the Narration Page ❑ Do the Scientific Demonstration: Water Flow ❑ Define bud and flower ❑ Work on memorizing the *Parts of a Flower* poem	❑ Read about Flowers and Pollen (or Flowering Plants, 2nd page) ❑ Add information to the weekly Narration Page ❑ Measure and record the growth of your plant for the Plant Growth Project ❑ Take the Plants Week 2 quiz

Five Days a Week Schedule				
❑ Read about Flowering Plants (or Flowering Plants, Intro) ❑ Add information on flowering plants to the Narration Page ❑ Do the Flowering Plants Project	❑ Read about Flowers (or Flowering Plants, 1st page) ❑ Add information on flowers to the Narration Page ❑ Do the Flowers Project	❑ Do the Scientific Demonstration: Water Flow ❑ Define bud and flower	❑ Read about Pollen (or Flowering Plants, 2nd page) ❑ Add information on pollen to the Narration Page ❑ Do the Pollen Project	❑ Take the Plants Week 2 quiz ❑ Measure and record the growth of your plant for the Plant Growth Project
All Week Long ❑ Work on memorizing the *Parts of a Flower* poem				

Notes

Week 3: Fruits and Seeds Lesson Plans

Scientific Demonstration: Baby Bean

Supplies Needed

- ✓ 4 or 5 dry pinto beans (**Note** — *You will need to pre-soak the beans for 24 hours before you do this scientific demonstration.*)
- ✓ Jar
- ✓ Paper towel

Purpose

This demonstration is meant to help the students identify the parts of the seed.

Instructions and Explanation

The instructions and explanation for this scientific demonstration are found on pp. 42-43 of *Janice VanCleave's Biology for Every Kid*. Have the students complete the Lab Report on SW pg. 81.

Take it Further

Repeat the demonstrations with several different types of seeds. Observe and discuss the similarities and differences.

Science-Oriented Books

Reading Assignments

- *Basher Biology pg. 123 (Fruit), pg. 122 (Seed)*
- *Usborne Science Encyclopedia pg. 274 (Seeds and Fruit)*

(Optional) Additional topic to explore this week: Seed Dispersal (USE pg. 276), Germination (USE pg. 277)

Discussion Questions

After reading the selected pages from the encyclopedias, ask the following questions in your discussion time:

Fruit

- ? Where does the fruit form?
- ? What does fruit do for the plant?

Seeds

- ? What does a seed contain?
- ? How are seeds moved around?

(Optional) Additional Books

- *Seeds* by Ken Robbins
- *From Seed to Plant* by Gail Gibbons
- *A Fruit Is a Suitcase for Seeds* by Jean Richards

- *From Seed to Apple (How Living Things Grow)* by Anita Ganeri
- *How a Seed Grows (Let's-Read-and-Find... Science 1)* by Helene J. Jordan
- *The Tiny Seed (World of Eric Carle)* by Eric Carle

Notebooking

Writing Assignments

- **Narration Page –** Have the students dictate, copy, or write one to four sentences on what they have learned about seeds and fruits on SW pg. 80. They can include information that they find interesting on each topic or material that you would like them to remember. (*See Plants Week 1 for a sample.*)
- **(Optional) Lapbook –** Have the students complete the Fruit Mini-book on pg. 56 from *Biology for the Grammar Stage Lapbooking Templates.* Have them begin by cutting out and coloring the mini-book. Then, ask the students what they have learned about fruit. Write their narration sentence on the inside of the book and have them glue the mini-book into the lapbook.
- **(Optional) Lapbook –** Have the students complete the Seeds Sheet on pg. 56 from *Biology for the Grammar Stage Lapbooking Templates.* Have them begin by cutting out and coloring the sheet. Then, have them label the seed on the sheet with radical and food store. (*The answer for this is provided on the right for your reference.*) Finally, glue the back of the sheet into the lapbook.

Parts of a Seed

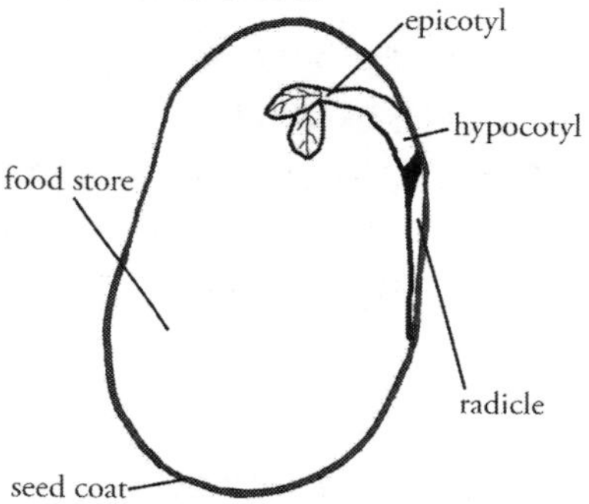

Vocabulary

The following definition is a guide. The students' definitions do not need to match word for word.

- **Seed –** The part of the plant that contains the beginnings of a new plant. (SW pg. 97)

Multi-week Projects and Activities

Unit Project

- **Plant Growth Project –** During this unit, the students will record the growth of a bean plant. This week, have them water the plant as necessary. On Friday, have them measure and record how much it has grown on the Plant Growth Record Chart on SW pg. 75.
- **(Optional) Nature Walk Sheets –** Each week, take a nature walk to look for flowers and unique leaves. If possible, have the students collect the leaves to take them home and press; if not, take a picture of the samples. Once you are back at home, have the students identify the flowers and leaves they found using a field guide book from the library or

the Internet. Have them record their findings on a Nature Walk Sheet found in the Appendix of this guide on pg. 198.

Projects for this Week

- ✂ **Coloring Pages –** You can have the students color the following pages from *Biology for the Grammar Stage Coloring Pages*: Fruit pg. 97, Seed pg. 98.
- ✂ **Fruit –** Have the students dissect a piece of fruit. You will need two pieces of fleshy fruit, such as an apple or orange, a knife, and a magnifying glass. Let the students observe the fruit. Does it look good? Does it smell good? Cut one of the fruits in half lengthwise, and cut the other in half widthwise. Let the students examine the fruit halves to locate the seeds and taste the flesh. Is the seed encased? Does the flesh surrounding the seed taste good? Be sure to point out the various parts of the fruit as they complete the dissection.
- ✂ **Seeds –** Go on a seed sock hunt. You will need a large field, a pair of tube socks per student, and a plastic bag. Have the students place the tube socks over their shoes and then walk through the field. Once the socks are covered with seeds, have them carefully remove the socks and place them in the plastic bag. After you get home, let the students observe the different seeds they collected and create a page to display them. If you have any older students, have them classify the seeds and identify how they are typically dispersed.

Memorization

- Work on memorizing the *Parts of a Flower* poem. (SW pg. 103)

<u>Parts of a Flower</u>
The bud becomes a flower
It's happening this very hour
The flower has petals so bright
It attracts the insect in flight
The stamen provides the pollen it needs
To join with the pistil and make a seed

Quiz

Weekly Quiz

- "Plants Unit Week 3 Quiz" on SW pg. Q-35.

Quiz Answers

1. True
2. Protect and disperse
3. Move seeds
4. Answers will vary

Notes

Possible Schedules for Week 3

Two Days a Week Schedule	
❑ Read about Seeds (or Intro and Inside a seed sections) ❑ Add information on seeds to the Narration Page ❑ Do the Scientific Demonstration: Baby Bean ❑ Define seeds ❑ Work on memorizing the *Parts of a Flower* poem	❑ Read about Fruits (or sections on Fruit) ❑ Add information to the weekly Narration Page ❑ Measure and record the growth of your plant for the Plant Growth Project ❑ Take the Plants Week 3 quiz

Five Days a Week Schedule				
❑ Read about Fruits ❑ Add information on fruit to the Narration Page ❑ Do the Fruit Project	❑ Read about Seeds (or Intro and Inside a seed sections) ❑ Add information on seeds to the Narration Page ❑ Do the Seeds Project	❑ Do the Scientific Demonstration: Baby Bean ❑ Define seeds	❑ Choose one or more of the additional books to read ❑ Take the Plants Week 3 quiz	❑ Measure and record the growth of your plant for the Plant Growth Project
All Week Long ❑ Work on memorizing the *Parts of a Flower* poem				

Week 4: Non-flowering Plants Lesson Plans

Scientific Demonstration: Inside the Cone

Supplies Needed

- ✓ Pine cone (tightly closed)
- ✓ Magnifying glass

Purpose

This demonstration is meant to help the students to learn more about a pine cone and where the seeds are located.

Instructions

1. Have the students examine the pine cone. Is it hard or soft? Is it sharp or dull?
2. Gently heat the pine cone in a 300°F oven until the scales open up. This should take less than five minutes. What do the students see now?
3. Have the students observe the pockets of space where the seeds normally rest. If there is a seed in one, have them take it out and examine it.
4. Have the students write their observations on their Lab Report on SW pg. 83.

Explanation

The cone is the delivery system and protector of the seeds for the conifer tree. As the cone and seeds mature, the scales are held tightly together. When the right conditions are present, the cone scales will open up and the seeds will be released.

Take it Further

Have the students place the pine cone in a glass of water and observe what happens. (*They should see that the pine cone closes.*)

Science-Oriented Books

Reading Assignments

- *Basher Biology pg. 30 (Seedless Plants), pg. 32 (Conifers), pg. 28 (Fungus)*
- *Usborne Science Encyclopedia pg. 275 (Cones), pp. 282-283 (Flowerless Plants), pp. 284-285 (Fungi)*

Discussion Questions

After reading the selected pages from the encyclopedias, ask the following questions in your discussion time:

Seedless Plants

- **?** How do seedless plants spread?
- **?** What types of plants are seedless ones?

Conifers

- **?** What is the job of a cone?
- **?** What types of plants are conifers?

Fungus

- **?** What does the fungus group include?
- **?** What is the job of fungus?

(Optional) Additional Books

- *Plants That Never Ever Bloom (Explore!)* by Ruth Heller
- *Ferns (Rookie Read-About Science)* by Allan Fowler
- *From Pine cone to Pine Tree* by Ellen Weiss
- *Fungi: Mushrooms, Toadstools, Molds, Yeasts, and Other Fungi* by Judy Wearing
- *Fungi (Kid's Guide to the Classification of Living Things)* by Elaine Pascoe and Janet Powell

Notebooking

Writing Assignments

- **Narration Page** – Have the students dictate, copy, or write one to four sentences on what they have learned for seedless plants, conifers, and fungus on SW pg. 82. They can include information that they find interesting on each topic or material that you would like them to remember. (*See Plants Week 1 for a sample.*)
- **(Optional) Lapbook** – Have the students complete the Seedless Plants Tab-book on pg. 57 from *Biology for the Grammar Stage Lapbooking Templates*. Have them cut out the pages of the tab-book. Ask them to tell you what they have learned about each of the different types of seedless plants. Write their narrations on each page of the tab-book. Then, have them color the pictures on each page before assembling the tab-book. Once the students have finished, glue the tab-book into the lapbook. (**Note** — *Fungus is not technically a plant. However, it makes the most sense to include it in this section for the elementary student.*)

Vocabulary

The following definition is a guide. The students' definitions do not need to match word for word.

- **Cone** – A type of dry fruit produced by a conifer. (SW pg. 92)

Multi-week Projects and Activities

Unit Project

- **Plant Growth Project** – During this unit, the students will record the growth of a bean plant. This week, have them water the plant as necessary. On Friday, have them measure and record how much it has grown on the Plant Growth Record Chart on SW pg. 75.
- **(Optional) Nature Walk Sheets** – Each week, take a nature walk to look for flowers and unique leaves. If possible, have the students collect the leaves to take them home and press; if not, take a picture of the samples. Once you are back at home, have the students identify the flowers and leaves they found using a field guide book from the library or the Internet. Have them record their findings on a Nature Walk Sheet found in the

Appendix of this guide on pg. 198.

Projects for this Week

- ✂ **Coloring Pages –** You can have the students color the following pages from *Biology for the Grammar Stage Coloring Pages*: Seedless Plants pg. 99, Conifers pg. 100, Fungi pg. 101.
- ✂ **Seedless Plants –** Have the students observe a fern frond. You can purchase one from the local florist or look for a fern plant while on a nature walk. Have them observe the frond and look for evidence of spores. If they find spores, have them collect some to look at under the microscope. If you are unable to do so, the following website has a good image of microscopic spores:
  - http://botany.thismia.com/2009/12/02/fern-life-cycle/
- ✂ **Conifers –** Have the students make a bird feeder from a pine cone. They will need will need string, peanut butter, and bird seed. Have them begin by tying string to the top of the pine cone so that it will hang on a branch. Then, have them slather the outside of the pine cone with peanut butter. After that, have them roll the cone in bird seed and hang it outside for the birds to enjoy.
- ✂ **Fungi –** Have the students watch the following National Geographic video about mushrooms:
  - https://www.youtube.com/watch?v=zb4y40kFhL4

Memorization

- Work on memorizing the *Parts of a Plant* poem. (SW pg. 103)

Parts of a Plant

The plant stem holds it up high
The leaves reach way up to the sky
It has roots that go into the ground
Gathering nutrients and keeping balance sound

Quiz

Weekly Quiz

- "Plants Unit Week 4 Quiz" on SW pg. Q-38.

Quiz Answers

1. Dry fruits
2. True
3. Mushrooms, Yeasts, Molds
4. Answers will vary

Notes

Possible Schedules for Week 4

Two Days a Week Schedule	
❑ Read about Conifers (or Cones) ❑ Add information on conifers to the Narration Page ❑ Do the Scientific Demonstration: Inside the Cone ❑ Define cone ❑ Work on memorizing the *Parts of a Plant* poem	❑ Read about Seedless Plants and Fungi (or Flowerless Plants and Fungi) ❑ Add information to the weekly Narration Page ❑ Measure and record the growth of your plant for the Plant Growth Project ❑ Take the Plants Week 4 quiz

Five Days a Week Schedule				
❑ Read about Seedless Plants (or Flowerless Plants) ❑ Add information on seedless plants to the Narration Page ❑ Do the Seedless Plants Project	❑ Read about Conifers (or Cones) ❑ Add information on conifers to the Narration Page ❑ Do the Conifer Project	❑ Do the Scientific Demonstration: Inside the Cone ❑ Define cone	❑ Read about Fungus (Fungi) ❑ Add information on fungi to the Narration Page ❑ Do the Fungi Project	❑ Take the Plants Week 4 quiz ❑ Measure and record the growth of your plant for the Plant Growth Project
All Week Long ❑ Work on memorizing the *Parts of a Plant* poem				

Week 5: Stems Lesson Plans

Scientific Demonstration: Stand Up

Supplies Needed

- ✓ 1 Glass
- ✓ A piece of wilted celery
- ✓ Blue food coloring

Purpose

This demonstration is meant to help the students to see how turgor pressure helps to hold the stem up.

Instructions and Explanation

The instructions and explanation for this scientific demonstration are found on pp. 14-15 of *Janice VanCleave's Biology for Every Kid*. Have the students complete the Lab Report on SW pg. 85.

Take it Further

Repeat the demonstration with several different colors of food coloring.

Science-Oriented Books

Reading Assignments

- *Basher Biology pg. 110 (Plant Cell), pg. 116 (Stem)*
- *Usborne Science Encyclopedia pp. 250-251 (Plant Cells), pg. 252 (Stems)*

Discussion Questions

After reading the selected pages from the encyclopedias, ask the following questions in your discussion time:

Plant Cells

- **?** What is the cell wall's purpose?
- **?** Name several of the organelles found in a plant cell.

Stems

- **?** What are two things that the stem does for the plant?
- **?** What is transported through the stem?

(Optional) Additional Books

- *Stems (Plant Parts)* by Vijaya Bodach
- *Plant Plumbing: A Book About Roots and Stems* by Susan Blackaby
- *Stems (World of Plants)* by John Farndon
- *Plant Cells and Life Processes (Investigating Cells)* by Barbara A. Somerville
- *Powerful Plant Cells (Microquests)* by Rebecca L Johnson and Jack Desrocher

Notebooking

Writing Assignments

- ☐ **Narration Page –** Have the students dictate, copy, or write one to four sentences on what they have learned for plant cells and stems on SW pg. 84. They can include information that they find interesting on each topic or material that you would like them to remember. (*See Plants Week 1 for a sample.*)
- ☐ **(Optional) Lapbook –** Have the students work on their Parts of a Plant Tab-book. For this week, have the student cut out and color the cover and stems page on pg. 52 from *Biology for the Grammar Stage Lapbooking Templates*. Ask the students what they have learned about stems this week and then add their narration to that page of the tab-book. Have them color the pictures on the sheet and save them until they assemble the booklet in the last week of the unit.
- ☐ **(Optional) Lapbook –** Have the students complete the plant cell sheet on pg. 53 from *Biology for the Grammar Stage Lapbooking Templates*. Have them color the plant cell and label the cell wall, cell membrane, nucleus, and chloroplasts. You can use the diagram provided as a guide to help your students label the plant cell.

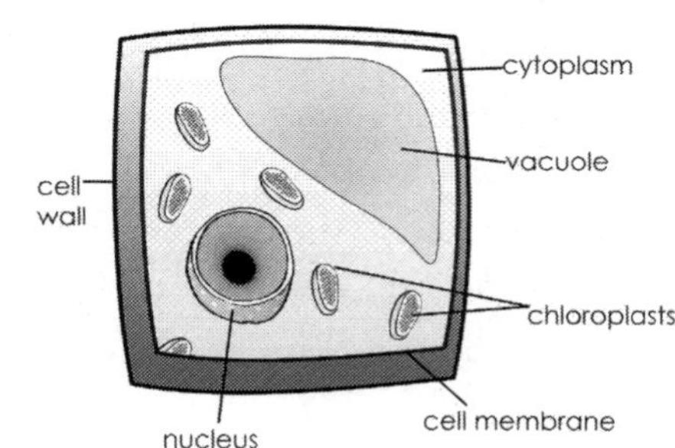

Vocabulary

The following definition is a guide. The students' definitions do not need to match word for word.

- **Stem –** The part of the plant that holds it upright and supports the leaves and flowers. (SW pg. 98)

Multi-week Projects and Activities

Unit Project

- ✂ **Plant Growth Project –** During this unit, the students will record the growth of a bean plant. This week, have them water the plant as necessary. On Friday, have them measure and record how much it has grown on the Plant Growth Record Chart on SW pg. 75.
- ✂ **(Optional) Nature Walk Sheets –** Each week, take a nature walk to look for flowers and unique leaves. If possible, have the students collect the leaves to take them home and press; if not, take a picture of the samples. Once you are back at home, have the students identify the flowers and leaves they found using a field guide book from the library or the Internet. Have them record their findings on a Nature Walk Sheet found in the Appendix of this guide on pg. 198.

Projects for this Week

- ✂ **Coloring Pages** – You can have the students color the following pages from *Biology for the Grammar Stage Coloring Pages*: Stem pg. 102, Plant Cell pg. 103.
- ✂ **Stems** – Have the students dissect a daffodil stem. For this project, you will need a daffodil, knife, and magnifying glass. Begin by having the students observe the stem with a magnifying glass. Then, cut the stem and look for the water droplets that begin to ooze out. Have the students examine the cut closely with the magnifying glass to look for the tubes. Discuss with the students what they are seeing as you go through the activity.
- ✂ **Plant Cell** – Have the students make a model of a plant cell. They will need Jell-O, green jelly beans, grapes, a banana slice, a small ziploc bag, and a small square plastic container. Begin by making the Jell-O according to the package directions and let it soft set. Have the students scoop a cup or two of lime Jell-O (the cytoplasm) into the ziploc baggie (the cell membrane). Next, have them place the organelles into their cytoplasm. The banana slice will serve as the nucleus, the grapes as the vacuoles, and the jelly beans as the chloroplasts. Once the students have placed the different organelles, have them remove the air, seal the baggie, and place it in the square container which acts as the cell wall. Then, place their models back into the fridge for another hour or so to set. After the plant cell models have set, take them out and let the students observe their creations.

Memorization

- Work on memorizing the *Parts of a Plant* poem. (SW pg. 103)

Parts of a Plant

The plant stem holds it up high
The leaves reach way up to the sky
It has roots that go into the ground
Gathering nutrients and keeping balance sound

Quiz

Weekly Quiz

- "Plants Unit Week 5 Quiz" on SW pg. Q-39.

Quiz Answers

1. Hold up flowers, Support the plant, Transport food and water
2. A. cell wall, B. chloroplasts, C. nucleus
3. Answers will vary

Notes

Possible Schedules for Week 5

Two Days a Week Schedule	
❑ Read about Stems (Stems) ❑ Add information on stems to the Narration Page ❑ Do the Scientific Demonstration: Stand Up ❑ Define stems ❑ Work on memorizing the *Parts of a Plant* poem	❑ Read about Plant Cells (or Plant Cells) ❑ Add information on plant cells to the weekly Narration Page ❑ Measure and record the growth of your plant for the Plant Growth Project ❑ Take the Plants Week 5 quiz

Five Days a Week Schedule				
❑ Read about Plant Cells (or Plant Cells) ❑ Add information on plant cells to the weekly Narration Page ❑ Do the Plant Cells Project	❑ Read about Stems ❑ Add information on stems to the Narration Page ❑ Do the Stems Project	❑ Do the Scientific Demonstration: Stand up ❑ Define stems	❑ Choose one or more of the additional books to read ❑ Take the Plants Week 5 quiz	❑ Measure and record the growth of your plant for the Plant Growth Project
All Week Long ❑ Work on memorizing the *Parts of a Plant* poem				

Week 6: Roots Lesson Plans

Scientific Demonstration: Grow a Bean

Supplies Needed

- ✓ Paper towels
- ✓ 4 Pinto Beans
- ✓ Masking tape
- ✓ One drinking glass
- ✓ Marking pen

Purpose

This demonstration is meant to help the students to determine if it matters how seeds are planted.

Instructions and Explanation

The instructions and explanation for this scientific demonstration are found on pp. 44-45 of *Janice VanCleave's Biology for Every Kid*. Have the students complete the Lab Report on SW pg. 87.

Take it Further

Repeat the demonstration with several different kinds of seeds to see if you get a different result. (*The students should see that their results were the same, no matter what kids of seed they grew.*)

Science-Oriented Books

Reading Assignments

- *Basher Biology pg. 117 (Roots)*
- *Usborne Science Encyclopedia pg. 253 (Roots)*
- *Types of Roots article on Appendix pg. 199*

(Optional) Coordinating topic to study this week: Fluid Movement *(from the Usborne Science Encyclopedia)*

Discussion Questions

After reading the selected pages from the encyclopedias, ask the following questions in your discussion time:

Roots

- ? What are two things that the roots do for the plant?

Types of Roots

- ? What are the two main types of roots?
- ? How do fibrous roots grow?
- ? How do taproots grow?

(Optional) Additional Books

- *What Do Roots Do?* by Kathleen V. Kudlinski
- *Roots (Plant Parts series)* by Vijaya Bodach

Notebooking

Writing Assignments

- Have the students dictate, copy, or write one to four sentences on what they have learned for roots and types of roots on SW pg. 86. They can include information that they find interesting on each topic or material that you would like them to remember. (*See Plants Week 1 for a sample.*)
- **(Optional) Lapbook –** Have the students work on their Parts of a Plant Tab-book. For this week, have the student cut out and color the cover and roots page on pg. 53 from *Biology for the Grammar Stage Lapbooking Templates*. Ask the students what they have learned about roots this week and then add their narration to that page of the tab-book. Have them color the pictures on the sheet, add the sheets they have done in the previous weeks, and staple the book together. Finally, have the students glue the tab-book into the lapbook.
- **(Optional) Lapbook –** Have the students cut out and color the "Parts of a Plant" poem on pg. 49 from *Biology for the Grammar Stage Lapbooking Templates*. Once they have finished, have them glue the poem into the lapbook.

Vocabulary

The following definition is a guide. The students' definitions do not need to match word for word.

- **Roots –** The part of the plant that anchors the plant firmly to the ground and absorbs water and nutrients. (SW pg. 96)

Multi-week Projects and Activities

Unit Project

- **Plant Growth Project –** This is the final week for this project. This week, have them water the plant as necessary. On Friday, have them measure and record how much it has grown on the Plant Growth Record Chart on SW pg. 75. After the students are finished, have them gently remove the plant from the pot and rinse the roots. Once it is clean, have them examine the root system of their bean plant up close.
- **(Optional) Nature Walk Sheets –** Each week, take a nature walk to look for flowers and unique leaves. If possible, have the students collect the leaves to take them home and press; if not, take a picture of the samples. Once you are back at home, have the students identify the flowers and leaves they found using a field guide book from the library or the Internet. Have them record their findings on a Nature Walk Sheet found in the

Appendix of this guide on pg. 198.

Projects for this Week

- ✂ **Coloring Page –** You can have the students color the following page from *Biology for the Grammar Stage Coloring Pages*: Roots pg. 104.
- ✂ **Review –** Sit down with the students several times this week to review what they have learned over the year.

Memorization

- Work on memorizing the *Parts of a Plant* poem. (SW pg. 103)

  Parts of a Plant

  The plant stem holds it up high
  The leaves reach way up to the sky
  It has roots that go into the ground
  Gathering nutrients and keeping balance sound

Quiz

Weekly Quiz

- "Plants Unit Week 6 Quiz" on SW pg. Q-40.

Quiz Answers

1. Fibrous root-grows out, Taproot-grows down
2. True
3. Strong
4. Answers will vary

Notes

Possible Schedules for Week 6

Two Days a Week Schedule	
❑ Read about Roots (Roots) ❑ Add information on roots to the Narration Page ❑ Do the Scientific Demonstration: Grow a Bean ❑ Define roots ❑ Work on memorizing the *Parts of a Plant* poem	❑ Read about Types of Roots ❑ Add information to the weekly Narration Page ❑ Measure and record the final growth of your plant for the Plant Growth Project ❑ Take the Plants Week 6 quiz ❑ Review the students' work from the year

Five Days a Week Schedule				
❑ Read about Roots (Roots) ❑ Add information on roots to the Narration Page ❑ Review the students' work from the year	❑ Do the Scientific Demonstration: Grow a Bean ❑ Define roots	❑ Read about the Types of Roots ❑ Add information on the types of roots to the Narration Page ❑ Review the students' work from the year	❑ Take the Plants Week 6 quiz ❑ Measure and record the final growth of your plant for the Plant Growth Project	❑ Review the students' work from the year
All Week Long ❑ Work on memorizing the *Parts of a Plant* poem				

Biology for the Grammar Stage

Appendix

Animal Diet Chart Placement Guide

The following suggestions are for placement on the Animal Diet Chart found on SW pp. 6-7. They are based on the food that the animal is most likely to eat.

Carnivore

- Chameleon
- Cheetah
- Crocodile
- Dolphin
- Eagle
- Fish
- Flamingo
- Frog
- Lion
- Octopus
- Owl
- Penguin
- Polar Bear
- Seahorse
- Shark
- Snake
- Spider
- Swallow
- Walrus
- Whale

Omnivore

- Ant
- Armadillo
- Chicken
- Chimpanzee
- Crab
- Duck
- Fox
- Ostrich
- Parrot
- Peacock
- Pig
- Shrimp
- Skunk
- Turtle
- Worm

Herbivore

- Beaver
- Butterfly
- Camel
- Cow
- Deer
- Elephant
- Giraffe
- Goat
- Grasshopper
- Hippo
- Hummingbird
- Iguana
- Kangaroo
- Koala
- Panda (see note)
- Parrot
- Rabbit
- Snail
- Swan
- Zebra

Note

The panda is officially classified as a carnivore, although its diet is vegetarian. Its digestive system is not well suited to its mainly bamboo diet. The intestines in a panda's gut are far too short to digest bamboo the way a typical herbivore would. In short, even though the panda has a diet like a herbivore, internally it more closely ressembles a carnivore. This is why they must eat such a vast quantity of the plant to survive. You can visit the Smithsonian website for more information on this:

http://nationalzoo.si.edu/Animals/GiantPandas/PandaFacts/

However, for the sake of this study, we have placed the panda under the herbivore size. The reason for this is because we are having the students classify the animals solely based on their diet and not their internal make-up. You can certainly discuss this issue with your students and place the panda under the carnivore section. If you do have an older student, I would recommend having this discussion with him.

Habitat Posters Placement Guide

The following suggestions are for placement on the following Habitat Posters. They are based on the habitat in which the animal is most likely to be found. Several of the animals can be found in multiple habitats, which is denoted by, " * ". This list is not all inclusive, it is merely meant to help you as you guide your students. If you discover that an animal can be found in another habitat and the students want to place them there instead, feel free to do so.

Woodland Forest

- Ant*
- Beaver
- Butterfly*
- Deer
- Duck*
- Eagle
- Fox*
- Frog*
- Grasshopper*
- Hummingbird*
- Koala
- Owl*
- Panda
- Rabbit
- Skunk
- Snake*
- Spider*
- Swallow*
- Swan*
- Worm*

Arctic

- Fox*
- Owl*
- Penguin
- Polar Bear
- Walrus
- Whale*

Domestic Farm

- Chicken
- Cow
- Goat
- Pig

Rainforest

- Alligator*
- Ant*
- Butterfly*
- Chameleon
- Chimpanzee
- Duck*
- Flamingo
- Grasshopper*
- Hippo
- Hummingbird*
- Iguana*
- Owl*
- Parrot
- Peacock
- Snake*
- Spider*
- Swallow*
- Worm*

Desert

- Ant*
- Armadillo
- Butterfly*
- Camel
- Crab*
- Fox*
- Grasshopper*
- Iguana*
- Ostrich*
- Owl*
- Snake*
- Spider*
- Worm*

Grassland

- Alligator*
- Ant*
- Butterfly*
- Cheetah
- Elephant
- Frog*
- Giraffe
- Grasshopper*
- Kangaroo
- Lion
- Ostrich*
- Owl*
- Snake*
- Spider*
- Swan*
- Worm*
- Zebra

Ocean

- Crab*
- Dolphin
- Fish
- Octopus
- Seahorse
- Shark
- Shrimp
- Whale*

Woodland Forest Habitat

Arctic Habitat

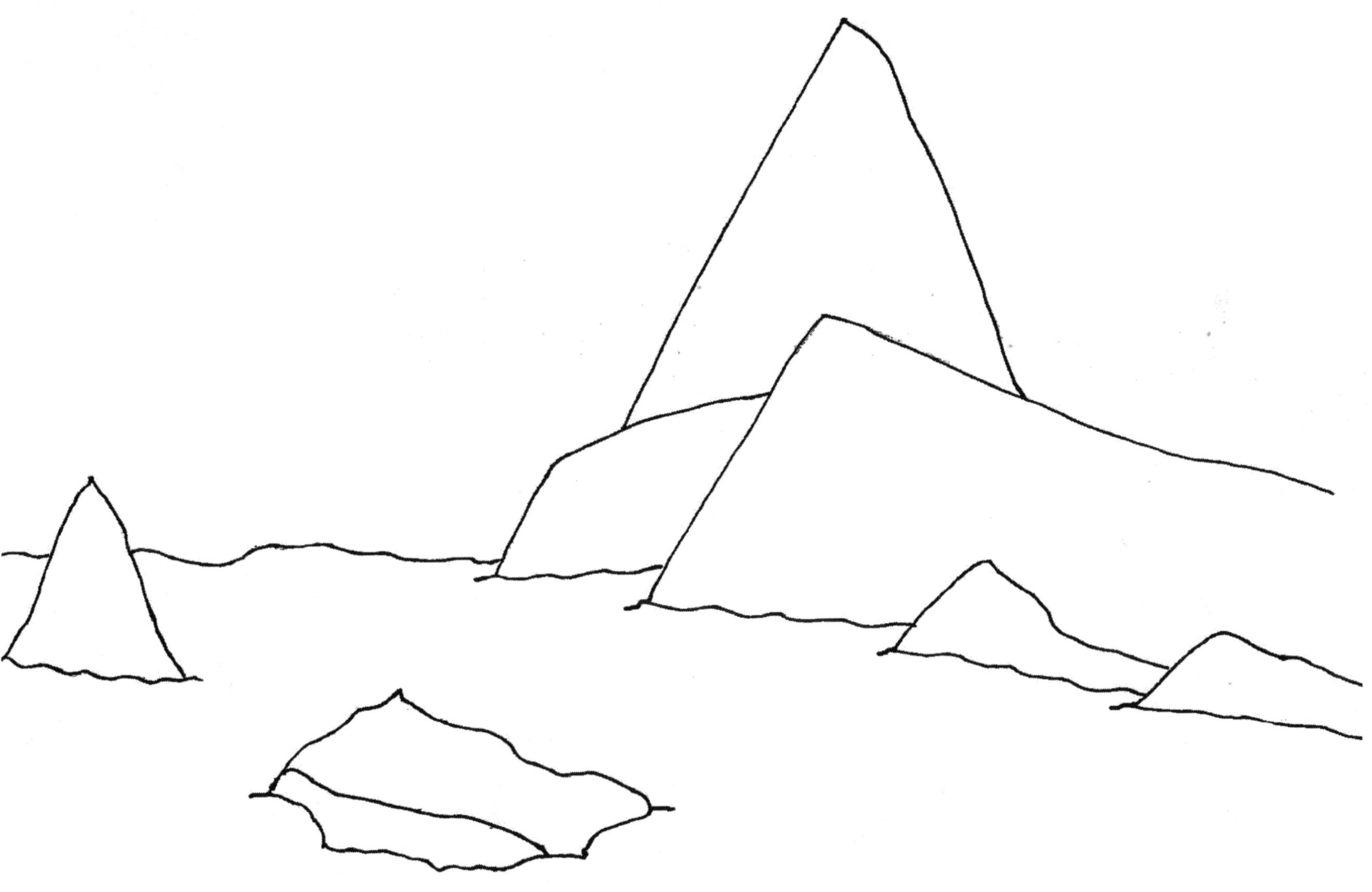

Domestic Farm Habitat

Rainforest Habitat

Desert Habitat

Grassland Habitat

Ocean Habitat

Animal Observation Sheet

Name of Animal: ____________________

Do I have a backbone?

Yes or No

Do I have fur?

Yes or No

Do I have wings?

Yes or No

What does my skin look like? ____________________

What does my body look like? ____________________

What do I eat? ____________________

What do my babies look like? ____________________

How many legs/feet do I have? ____________________

Where do I live? ____________________

Do I travel anywhere? ____________________

What size am I? ____________________

How do I defend myself? ____________________

What is special about me? ____________________

____

My Bird Feeder Book

Paste a picture of your bird feeder here.

By: ______________________________

Today I saw a ________________________ visit my bird feeder. This is what it looked like:

Paste or draw a picture of the bird you saw here.

Date: ______________________________

Today I saw a ____________________
visit my bird feeder. This is what it looked like:

Paste or draw a picture of the bird you saw here.

Date: ____________________

Today I saw a ____________________
visit my bird feeder. This is what it looked like:

Paste or draw a picture of the bird you saw here.

Date: ____________________

Chameleon

Butterfly Life Cycle Cards

Butterflies lay eggs on leaves.

Caterpillars hatch out of the eggs and eat the leaves.

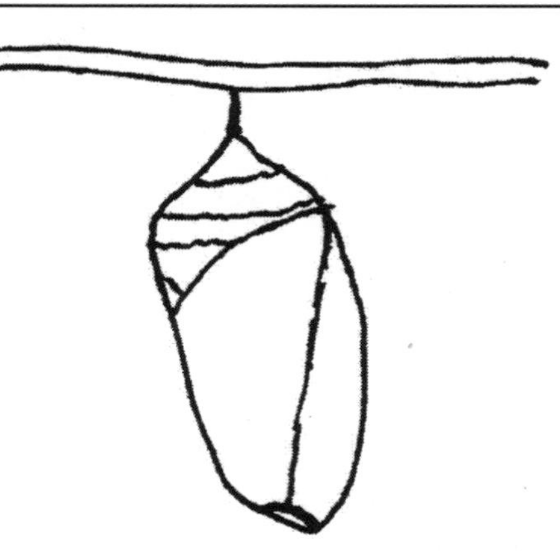

When they are full, caterpillars make a chrysalis.

A butterfly emerges from the chrysalis.

Microscope Worksheet

What I Looked At

____

____

What I Saw

____

____

____

____

____

____

____

____

____

My Drawing

Magnification Power ______x

Magnification Power ______x

Body Organization Cards

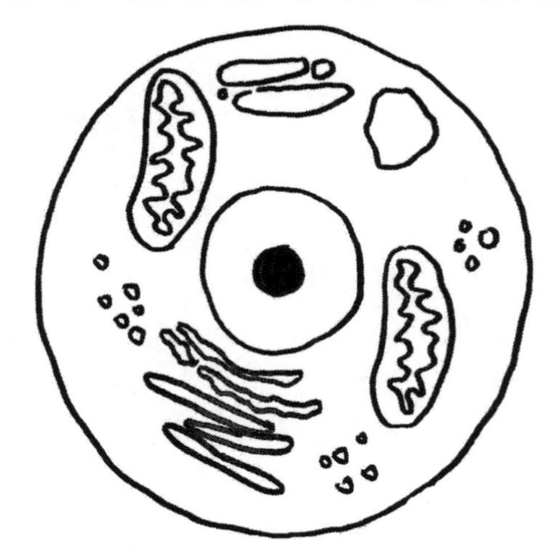

Cells are the smallest living units in the body.

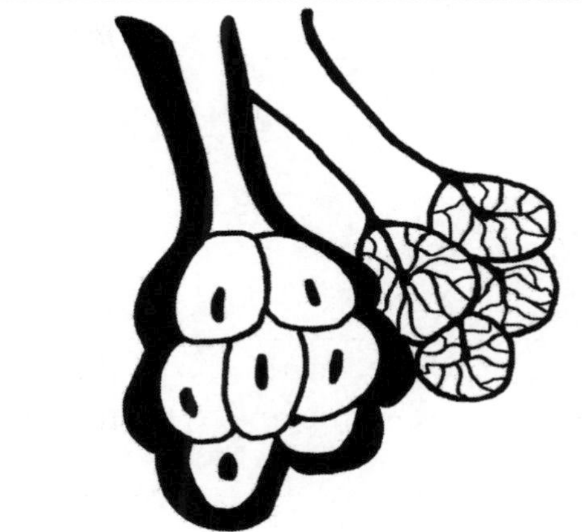

Cells that have the same job join together to form tissues.

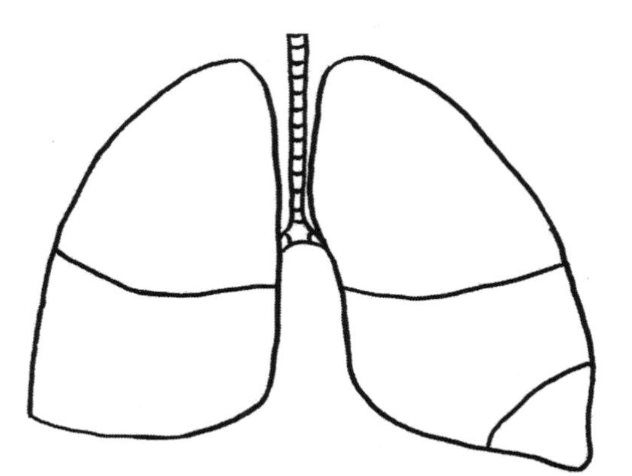

Several different types of tissues work together to make an organ.

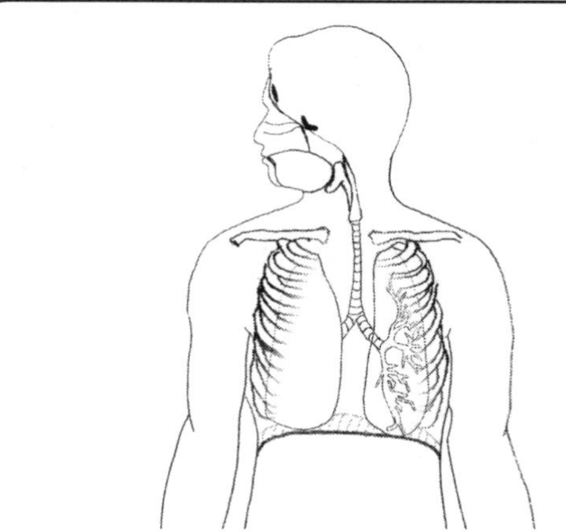

Organs work together in a system to perform the functions of the body.

Joints Project Directions

Pivot Joint

Supplies Needed

- ✓ A brad
- ✓ Card stock
- ✓ Scissors
- ✓ Hole Punch

Instructions

Cut two rectangles out of the card stock. Then, punch a hole at the end of each of the rectangles. Use the brad to fasten the two together to create a working pivot joint.

Hinge Joint

Supplies Needed

- ✓ 2 Lengths of 1x2 boards
- ✓ ½" hinge
- ✓ Several screws
- ✓ Screwdriver

Instructions

Lay the two boards end to end. Open the hinge and lay it across the point at which the boards meet. Use the screws and screwdriver to attach a side of the hinge to each of the boards. Once it is secure, you can open and shut the boards just like a hinge joint.

Ball and Socket Joint

Supplies Needed

- ✓ 1 Length of ½"plastic pipe
- ✓ 1 Length of ¾" plastic pipe
- ✓ 1 ½" Plastic pipe tee
- ✓ 1 ¾" Plastic pipe tee
- ✓ Pipe saw
- ✓ 2 Rubber bands

Instructions

Use the pipe saw to cut the top of the ¾" tee in half so that it forms a cup. Fit the ¾" pipe into the cut ¾" tee. Fit the ½" pipe into the ½" tee. Now fit the ½" tee into the cup of the cut ¾" tee. Use the two rubber bands to secure the two tees together and create a working ball and socket joint.

Pathways of Blood Worksheet

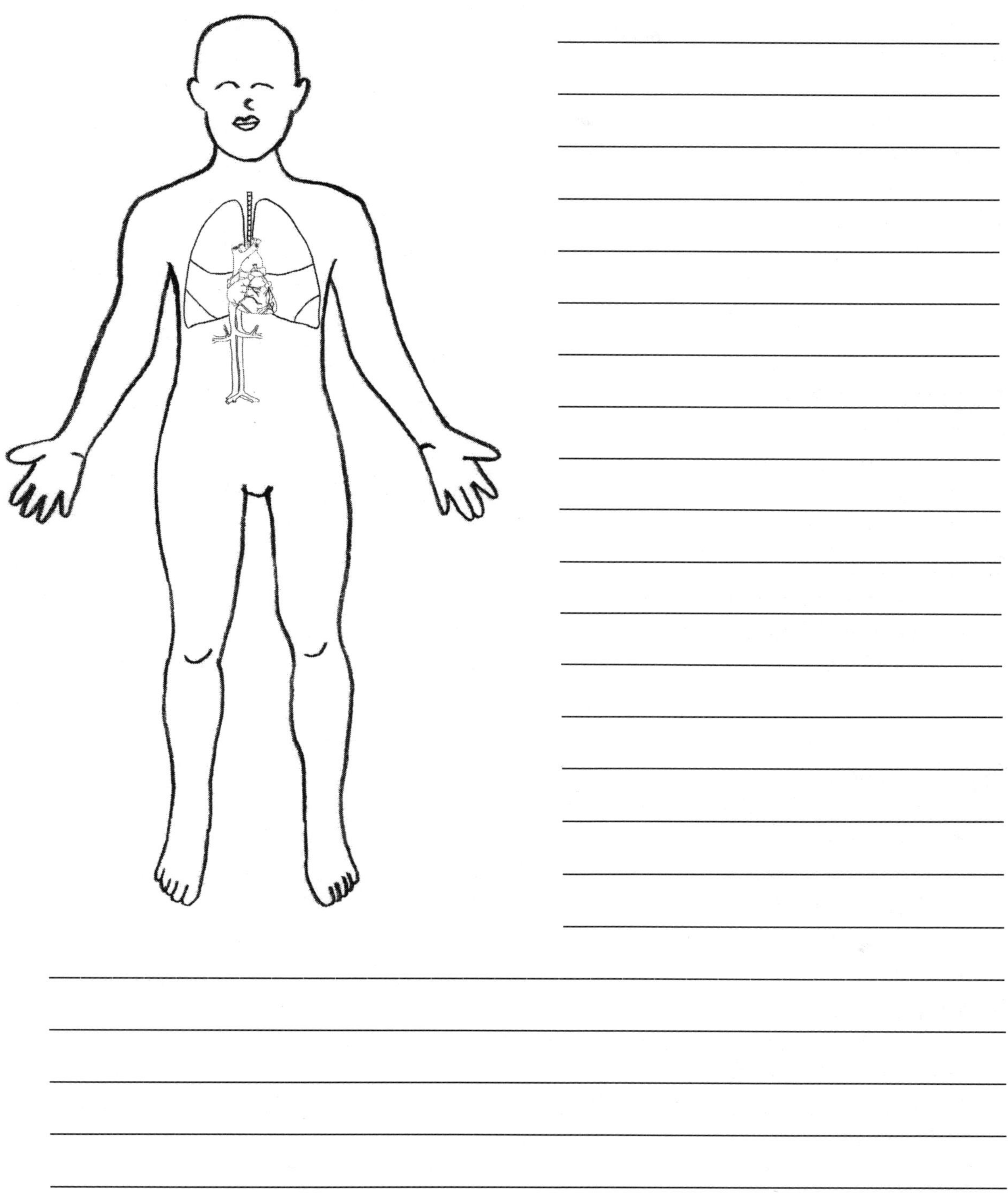

Inhalation vs. Exhalation Worksheet

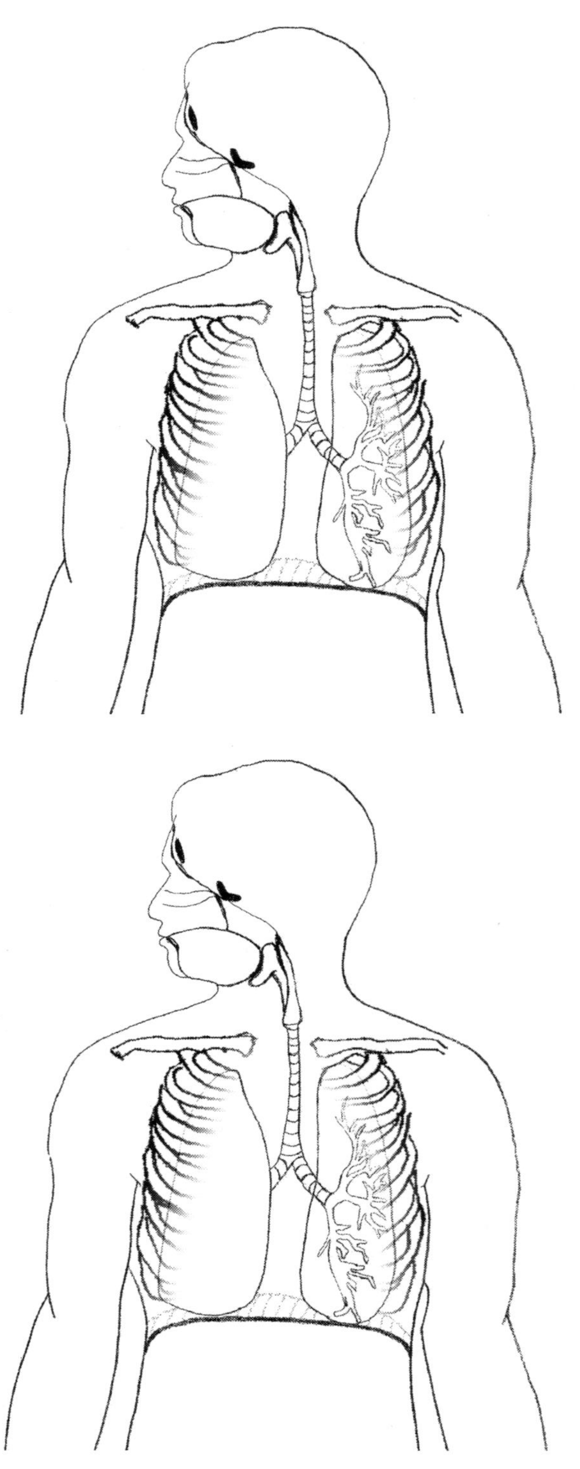

The Small Intestines vs. The Large Intestines

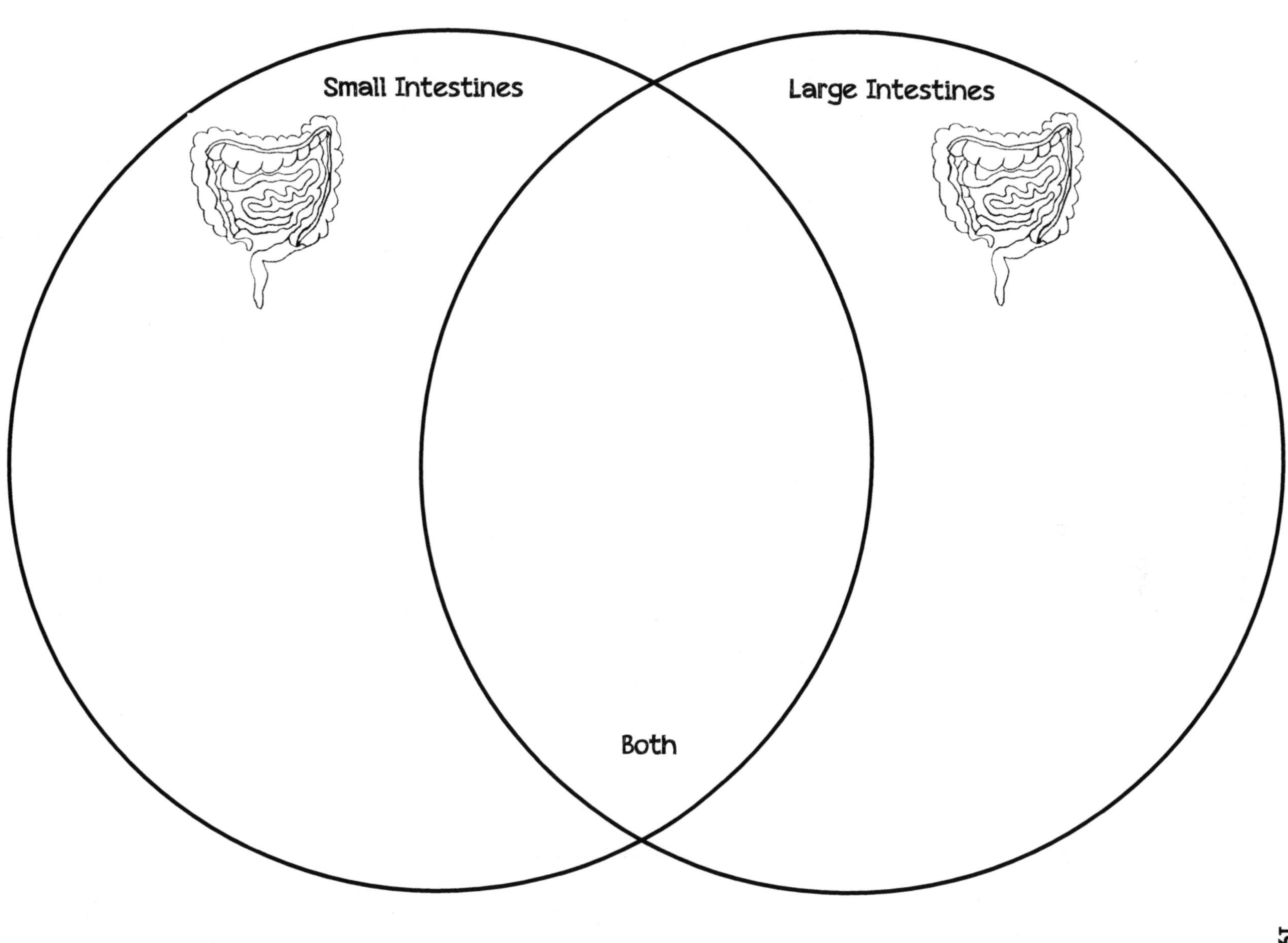

Nature Walk Sheet

Type of plant the flower or leaf came from: ______________________________

Where I found it: ____

____

Color of the flower or leaf: ____

Size of the flower or leaf: ____

Press the flower and leaf here or
paste a picture of it in this box.

Types of Roots

Roots are important to plants. They help to anchor the plant to the ground and to take in the water and nutrients the plant needs. As the roots of a plant grow, they will spread out as far as they can to reach as much water as possible.

Plants have two basic types of roots – fibrous and taproots. These are classified by how the roots develop and branch out.

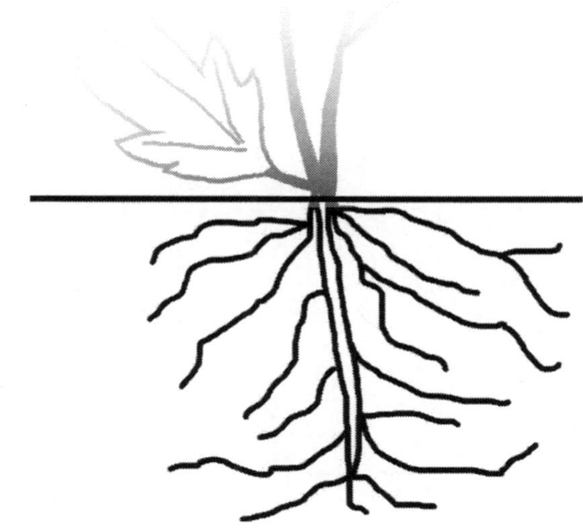

Fibrous roots are the most common root types. These roots are all about the same size, meaning that there is not a large single root in the center. Fibrous roots branch out multiple times as they grow. Plants with fibrous roots will have a mass of similarly sized roots at their base. The grass in your yard is a good example of a plant with fibrous roots.

Taproots, on the other hand, develop a single central root that is faster and deeper than the other branches. Plants with taproots have a large primary root with smaller rootlets that develop off of the main root. The dandelion in your yard is a good example of a plant with a taproot.

Biology for the Grammar Stage

Glossary

A

- **Alveoli –** Tiny air bags found in your lungs.
- **Amphibian –** A cold-blooded, smooth-skinned vertebrate, such as a frog or salamander.

B

- **Bacteria –** A group of microscopic organisms that can cause diseases.
- **Bird –** A warm-blooded, egg-laying, feathered vertebrate; it also has wings.
- **Blood vessel –** A tube that carries blood through the body.
- **Bud –** A swelling on a plant stem containing tiny flower parts ready to burst into a bloom.

C

- **Carnivore –** An animal that feeds on other animals.
- **Cell –** A tiny, living unit that is the building block of all living things.
- **Cone –** A type of dry fruit produced by a conifer.

D

- **Digestion –** The process by which your food is broken down.
- **Domesticated Animal –** An animal that has been under human control for many generations.

E

- **Egg –** The reproductive structure of some animals.

F

- **Fish –** A cold-blooded, aquatic vertebrate with gills and fins; it typically also has an elongated body covered with scales.
- **Flower –** The reproductive parts of a plant.

G

H

- **Habitat –** The natural environment of a plant or animal; a place that is natural for the life and growth of an animal or plant.
- **Herbivore –** An animal that feeds on plants.

I

- **Insect –** An invertebrate animal that has three body parts (head, thorax, and abdomen) and six legs.

- **Invertebrate –** An animal without a backbone.

J

K

- **Kidney –** The organ in the body responsible for removing waste from itself and regulating the body's fluid levels.

L

- **Leaf –** The part of the plant that makes the food for the plant.

M

- **Mammals –** Any warm-blooded vertebrate with skin that is more or less covered with hair; they give birth to live young that are nourished with milk at the beginning of their life.
- **Marine Mammal –** An animal that has all the characteristics of a mammal, but that also lives in the water.
- **Migration –** A journey made by an animal to a new habitat.
- **Muscle –** A type of tissue that makes the bones of your body move and that is controlled by your brain.

N

- **Neuron –** A nerve cell that makes up the nervous system and carries electrical messages throughout the body.

O

- **Omnivore –** An animal that feeds both on plants and animals.

P

Q

R

- **Reptile –** A group of cold-blooded animals that usually have rough skin.
- **Roots –** The part of the plant that anchors the plant firmly to the ground and absorbs water and nutrients.

S

- **Seed –** The part of the plant that contains the beginnings of a new plant.
- **Senses –** The ability of the body to take in and respond to information from its surroundings.
- **Shellfish –** An aquatic invertebrate animal with a shell.
- **Skeleton –** The framework of 206 bones that supports your body; it allows you to move and protects certain organs.
- **Stem –** The part of the plant that holds it upright and supports the leaves and flowers.

T

U

V

- **Vertebrate –** An animal with a backbone.

W

- **Wild Animal –** An animal that is typically found only in the wild.

X

Y

Z

Biology for the Grammar Stage

General Templates

Project Record Sheet

Paste a picture of your project in this box.

What I Learned:

____

____

____

____

____

____

____

____

Two Days a Week Schedule

Day 1	Day 2
❑	❑
❑	❑
❑	❑
❑	❑
❑	❑
❑	❑

Things to Prepare

- ❑
- ❑
- ❑

Notes

Five Days a Week Schedule

Day 1	Day 2	Day 3	Day 4	Day 5
❑	❑	❑	❑	❑
❑	❑	❑	❑	❑
❑	❑	❑	❑	❑
❑	❑	❑	❑	❑

All Week Long

❑

❑

Things to Prepare

❑

❑

❑

Notes

Made in the USA
Columbia, SC
27 September 2018